RMS MAJESTIC

'Building the *Bismarck*, Hamburg, Germany, 1914.' This lithograph was produced by American artist Joseph Pennell (1857–1926). (*Süddeutsche Zeitung*/Alamy Stock Photo)

RMS MAJESTIC

THE 'MAGIC STICK'

MARK CHIRNSIDE

The
History
Press

Cover illustrations
Front: This illustration graced a stylish brochure shortly after the Cunard White Star merger. The new company portrayed a ship which was, in some ways, a mix of both *Berengaria* and *Majestic* – the original had the three funnels coloured in a deep Cunard red rather than the lighter White Star 'buff'. It has been edited to reflect the White Star colour. (Author's collection).
Rear: Majestic's funnels project an image of power that was entirely accurate. (Author's collection)

First published 2006
This edition published 2024

The History Press
97 St George's Place, Cheltenham,
Gloucestershire, GL50 3QB
www.thehistorypress.co.uk

British Library Cataloguing in Publication Data.
A catalogue record for this book is available from the British Library.

ISBN 978 1 80399 337 9

Typesetting and origination by The History Press
Printed in Turkey by Imak

Trees for Life

CONTENTS

Acknowledgements 7

Introduction 8

1 The Anglo-German Century 9

2 Building a Giantess 15

3 Hamburg: 'City of Silence' 25

4 Sweet Success 55

5 The Peak Years 77

6 An Emptying Ocean 87

7 HMS *Caledonia* 119

Appendices 136

Appendix 1: British Registry Details of *Majestic* 136

Appendix 2: *Majestic* Particulars of Interest 137

Appendix 3: 'Some Interesting Features' 138

Appendix 4: *Majestic* & *Berengaria* Profits and Losses 139

Appendix 5: *Majestic* Passenger Statistics 141

Notes 142

Bibliography 144

Bismarck's mighty hull was the heaviest yet when she was launched in June 1914. (Artokoloro/Alamy Stock Photo)

ACKNOWLEDGEMENTS

This book was a team effort, as they always are. I owe my thanks to so many people, who helped with both the first edition and this revised and expanded edition. Family and friends encouraged and put up with me. Many people freely shared their expertise, information and source material:

Scott Andrews; Mark Baber; Günter Bäbler; Bruce Beveridge; Dawn Brooker and Keith Harrington; Bob Cullum; John Creamer; Jim Duckworth; Richard de Kerbrech; Neal Ditchett; David Hume Elkington; Ioannis Georgiou; Brent Holt; Brian Hawley; Jim Kalafus; Daniel Klistorner; J. Kent Layton; Peter Leach; Eric Longo; Campbell McCutcheon; Frank Melville; Jeff Newman; Eric Sauder; Michael Schneider; Richard Sloan; Geoff Swinfield; Johnstone White; Sheila Orysiek.

The staff of the British Library; Aaron Schmidt and the staff of the Boston Public Library; the staff of the Special Collections and Archives (Cunard), at Liverpool University's Sydney Jones Library; Halifax Herald Ltd; the staff of the Internationales Maritimes Museum Hamburg; Jim Duckworth and colleagues from the *Majestic Caledonia* Boys Association 1937–39; the staff of the Merseyside Maritime Museum archives; National Archives & Records Administration, Washington (NARA); Jonathan Ferguson and the staff of the National War Museum, Edinburgh Castle (National Museums Scotland); the staff of Public Record Office Northern Ireland (PRONI); Vicky Green and the staff at Southampton City Library, Archives & Information Services; the staff of the United Kingdom National Archives (formerly the Public Record Office). To anyone I have inadvertently left out, I can only offer my apologies and promise that this oversight will be corrected when the opportunity arises.

Any errors are solely my responsibility and I welcome any corrections supported by documentation. One particular area where records can differ is in the number of passengers carried by *Majestic* (I have relied largely on the North Atlantic Passenger Conference's tables showing the ship's total yearly passenger carryings). There are some minor discrepancies between these and the Conference's individual tables. In the appendices, I also noted the differences found in financial records from White Star and Cunard, then the records of the merged company.

Last but not least, my grateful thanks again to my publisher and everyone involved with both editions: For the first edition: Campbell McCutcheon, editors Leafy Robinson and Emily Pearce, cover designer Katie Beard and page setter Viktor Yordanov. For the new edition: commissioning editor Amy Rigg, project editor Jezz Palmer, designer Jem Cox and cover designer Martin Latham.

INTRODUCTION

Majestic's life and times were remarkable. Launched as *Bismarck* for Albert Ballin's HAPAG a few weeks before the start of the First World War, she lay idle throughout the conflict. Following Germany's defeat, she was allocated to the United Kingdom and the White Star Line acquired her from the British government. Her new name, *Majestic*, earned her the affectionate nickname 'The Magic Stick'. Throughout the 1920s, she was a great success. She was often the most popular liner on the North Atlantic run. Unfortunately, the Depression of the 1930s brought tough economic times and she was withdrawn from service in 1936, after the merger of the Cunard and White Star Lines to form a single strong British company on the North Atlantic. It was then that she was saved from the scrapyard by the British government, who needed to use her as a naval training ship. She served as HMS *Caledonia* until a serious fire in September 1939 signalled her demise. Her scrapping provided material to support the British war effort.

Hers was a short commercial lifespan for such an impressive vessel: she only saw fourteen years of service as a passenger liner, and not for the company or country who had constructed her. The first edition of *RMS Majestic: The 'Magic Stick'* was the first book to cover her history in its own right, but it sold out quickly and has been out of print since shortly after publication in 2006. This revised and expanded edition has been increased from 96 to 144 pages, supplemented by many rare and previously unpublished illustrations. There is a lot of new material covering her period as HMS *Caledonia*. Hers is an interesting history, from the great successes to the failures, under three names and three owners.

1

THE ANGLO-GERMAN CENTURY

'The largest ship afloat, the 50,000-ton *Imperator*, steamed *majestic*ally up the harbour from Quarantine yesterday forenoon to her pier in Hoboken', wrote the *New York Times* on 20 June 1913. 'From the time she hove anchor at 9.20 a.m. until her pier was reached at 11.12 a.m. the *Imperator*'s progress was marked by volleys of cheers from passengers on ferryboats and sight-seeing yachts and by a succession of shrill blasts from every kind of craft in New York …' She had not encountered any ice, but the press reported that she diverted to the south: *Olympic*'s Captain Haddock had warned 'that he had sighted two small bergs'. The new leviathan made her maiden voyage little more than a year after the *Titanic* disaster, displacing *Olympic* as the largest liner in the world. Alexander Carlisle was on board. He had spent decades working for Harland & Wolff and had a leading hand in the design of so many of the greatest ships built, so his praise was all the more noteworthy: 'The ship surpassed any other I have seen on three points: the Ritz-Carlton restaurant, with its palm garden on the deck; the wonderful swimming bath, which is modelled after that of the Royal Automobile Club in London, and the ballroom …' The weather was 'either rough or foggy for practically the entire trip' and she only ran one day at full speed. Even then, six of the forty-six boilers were not in use.

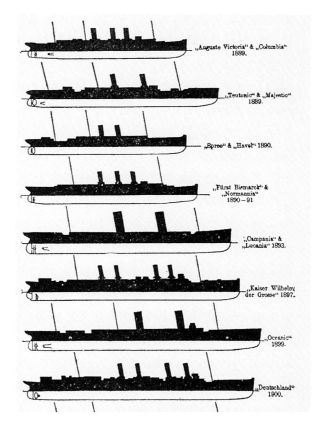

'A Chart of Progress in Steamship Construction.' White Star's *Oceanic*, HAPAG's *Deutschland* and Norddeutscher Lloyd's *Kaiser Wilhelm II* entered service within a few years of each other. *Oceanic* had never been intended to be the fastest liner afloat and *Deutschland* marked the last time that HAPAG sought the distinction. (Unknown journal, *c.*1901/Georgiou/Chirnside/Klistorner/Layton collection)

Norddeutscher Lloyd's *Kaiser Wilhelm der Grosse*, illustrated in an article about 'Ocean Record Breakers' by F.L. Finck. Her success in 1897 marked the start of a decade where the Blue Riband was in German hands. (*Metropolitan Magazine*, 1897/Georgiou/Chirnside/Klistorner/Layton collection)

Ballin's British rivals were keen to assess the new ship. Cunard's Leonard Peskett and C.W. Garrard had joined her on 11 June 1913 at Cuxhaven, staying on board for her call at Southampton on the afternoon of 12 June 1913 and until her arrival at Cherbourg that evening. They took notes: 'The ship was moored in a sheltered spot a little to the eastward of the mouth of the Elbe' and passengers were 'conveyed to the vessel by tender'. *Imperator*'s 'general outline' was 'far from being smart. There is an appearance of bulk, and a lack of continuity in the fairness of the sight lines of the superstructure. The bow and stern are heavy and similar in character to a full lined cargo ship.' They thought 'insufficient time had been allowed for the satisfactory completion of the ship. The staff were wearied out and suffering from loss of nerve. Herr Ballin had given orders that the ship was to sail on the eleventh, and his instructions were obeyed, but in every part of the ship there was no lack of the signs of haste – decks in many places were off the saw, paint thrown on, furniture half

polished, fittings broken, bad joints in plumbing everywhere …' Four thousand workmen had been aboard since the trial trip and all 'had to be housed and fed on board': 'The builder's representative informed us, in strict confidence, that they had lost [money] heavily on the contract. The wages for the men amounted to £10,000 per week for the eight weeks that the ship had been lying outside the harbour.' HAPAG officials found 'that the ship was very tender', meaning she had insufficient stability.

They wrote that there were 1,223 crew, including a navigating staff of one commander; one staff captain for ship supervision; three navigating captains – one for each watch; and seven officers. Unfortunately the stewards were berthed near the firemen: 'one cannot expect a steward to go on duty in a clean condition when he lives in a room where firemen are continually coming up from below shaking the coal dust from their clothes in the alleyway adjacent his room'. In the passenger accommodation, electric bells had been installed by Siemens & Halske, Berlin: 'at each bed and sofa seat there are two pushes, one red and one green, red for steward, green for stewardess …' The light stayed on until the call had been answered. The ventilation could be improved: 'compartments below the superstructure are warm and stuffy'. On the other hand, they were very impressed by much of the ship. The first-class lounge was 'undoubtedly the masterpiece of the vessel; the general proportions are extraordinary'. The 'scheme of decoration is Louis XIV. The models were selected in Paris and sent to Heimann of Berlin, who carried out the work. The walls are panelled with richly carved oak with large casement windows extending through two decks. Two pieces of antique Beauvais tapestry are hung on each side; they blend very harmoniously with the woodwork.' Then there was the 'beautifully proportioned' palm court with its grey-panelled walls 'and gilt trellis Louis VXI style with a large lay light in centre clouded blue, ceiling at the sides'. The 'corridors and alleyways' were all 'laid with rubber cork tiling light brown with blue lines …' The Turkish and electric bath arrangement was 'very suitable for ship work'. The second-class dining saloon was decorated in Adam style 'with carved ornament painted shades of grey … seating accommodation is provided for 436 persons'. Third-class accommodation was 'excellent'. The third-class dining saloon was 'treated more decoratively than usual. The bulkhead covered with vertical panels with decorated stiles; panelled ceilings; mahogany chairs leather covered; tables covered with table cloth'. Third-class staterooms were 'a good size and well ventilated'. Fourth class consisted of 'portable cabins for all married folk and single women, similar to portable third class. Open berths for all single men. Dining tables in covered shelter deck promenade.'

She entered service at a time of prosperity. In 1913, HAPAG carried 212,921 passengers on its Hamburg to New York service, up from 171,346 passengers in 1912 and 133,973 in 1911. From 1907 to 1913 inclusive, their German rival NDL carried 1,357,397 passengers on its New York services and HAPAG carried 1,119,870; the British lines, White Star and Cunard, carried 907,138 and 884,769 passengers respectively. The German lines were particularly strong with third-class westbound passengers. Although HAPAG lagged NDL in overall passenger numbers, their average number of passengers carried per crossing was higher. It was almost as good as its British rivals, standing at almost 1,400 passengers instead of under 1,000 for NDL. *Imperator* did more than her share in 1913, carrying 35,923 passengers at an average of 2,566 passengers per crossing.

HAPAG's success was in no small part due to Ballin's work. As the head of their North Atlantic Passenger Division since 1886, he proved his worth and rose to managing director. [1] Following their experience with the speedy *Deutschland* in the early 1900s, they had eschewed record-breaking speed in favour of comfort and economy of operation. *Amerika* (1905) was a prime example. In 1907, *Deutschland* averaged 746 passengers per crossing on the Hamburg to New York express service. *Amerika* operated a 'regular service' on the same route and averaged 1,850 passengers, with her daily coal consumption reported as almost 60 per cent less than *Deutschland*'s. She carried more passengers and burned less coal, which made for a compelling commercial proposition. By taking this approach, HAPAG were following behind the White Star Line, who were already planning two huge new liners (the first to surpass 40,000 gross tons) to be followed by a third. They had moved their express ships to Southampton in 1907, helping them to compete for the continental passenger traffic to and from New York. The fastest liners afloat in 1907 were Cunard's new *Lusitania* and *Mauretania*, but their construction had only been financially viable with state support. Rivals simply could not compete on speed. Indeed, NDL's *George Washington* (completed in 1909) prioritised passenger comfort and economy of operation. She was one of the largest ships in the world but her speed put her firmly behind NDL's express liners built ten years earlier.

As it turned out, 1907 came to a close with an economic downturn in the United States. On 4 October 1908, the *New York Times* reported that Ballin had been concerned about 'the costliness of Atlantic trade, owing to competition' and that 'his suggestion that $10,000,000 [£2,000,000] a year could be saved by the competition lines if a common agreement could be arrived at, have aroused keen interest in shipping circles here'. The article noted: 'all the companies realise that millions are being lost by the overlapping of sailings and by other unnecessary forms of competition, which must, in the view of many, inevitably result in disaster'. However, with Cunard's *Lusitania* and *Mauretania* in service and White Star's new ships on the way, one steamship manager said he could not 'think for a moment' that Cunard or White Star would 'ever consent to enter a combine in which they would be compelled to sail in stated rotation with other much less speedy ships'. On the other hand, NDL's Dr Weigand had been more optimistic about passenger travel, saying that 'the time was coming when even the enlarged fleet of his company would again be found too small …' Early in March 1909, *Shipping Gazette and Lloyd's List* noted that HAPAG was not going to pay any dividend at all for 1908 (it had already fallen between 1905 and 1907). HAPAG's gross profits in 1908 were down 50 per cent compared to 1906:

> The directors refer to the deadly competition forced upon the German lines by the *Lusitania* and *Mauretania*. 'The construction of these record-breaking vessels', says the company's statement, 'had and still has a most disastrous influence upon the shipping trade … The commissioning of the new Cunard giants awakens a natural desire to build equally large or larger vessels, for the shipping companies deal with that international public which seeks the most comfortable and luxuriously furnished ships. The fact cannot be concealed that the necessity to construct giant vessels has precipitated an era of most over-burdensome expense.

The British press had no sympathy. 'When Herr Ballin complains that an era of most burdensome expense has been precipitated, we must remember that the director-general of the Hamburg-American Line has by his own actions done much to stimulate Atlantic luxury.' Nobody doubted that HAPAG 'will recover'.

Several years earlier, Ballin had ordered the construction of *Europa* from the Belfast shipbuilding firm Harland & Wolff. She was intended to be 715ft in length between perpendiculars (at the waterline) and 80ft in breadth with a service speed of 17.5 knots, but design changes were soon in the works. The power of her engines was increased. Her speed was amended to 18 and then 18.5 knots. On 13 September 1906,

the shipyard and engine works were 'ordered to proceed' but a 'superseding order' was issued before the end of November 1906, apparently cancelling the work. The intended delivery date was April 1909 but, in the end, she was never completed and her Yard Number 391 was reassigned.

Ballin decided to 'compete on two fronts. On the one hand, he clearly wanted to challenge in the cabin and first class passenger business against the spate of fast British luxury liners constructed … On the other hand, HAL [HAPAG] would compete in all classes of passengers and express freight against Lloyd [NDL]'.[2] HAPAG's financial health had recovered to such an extent that Ballin was able to raise sufficient funds for substantial new tonnage, enough to put rival NDL 'in serious danger of losing its position' on the North Atlantic. His plans for three enormous liners led to the design of three ships whose 'passenger carrying capacity almost equalled that' of HAPAG's existing North Atlantic fleet. During the 'boom years of 1911–13' Ballin's 'ambitions knew no bounds'. Accordingly, plans took shape for three huge liners that would become the largest and most luxurious in the world, surpassing 50,000 gross tons for the first time. In the summer of 1910, *Europa* (later *Imperator*) was laid down at Vulcanwerke's Hamburg shipyard; in September 1911, a second ship (launched as *Vaterland*) was laid down as Yard Number 212 at Blohm & Voss' shipyard in Hamburg.[3] Early in December 1911, Ballin had seen press reports that White Star had ordered 'another steamer of the "*Olympic*" type'. He suggested to their chairman J. Bruce Ismay that it would be a 'wise policy if we agree not to exceed certain dimensions. Propose 900 feet by 100 feet. We are discussing contract for a third boat of this type, and shall probably have to order a fourth ship like that within [the] next six months to secure a weekly service from April 1915. Think it does not pay to continue this race for the largest ship.' His ships were going to be larger: Ballin wanted to stop the race after he had won it.

THE GREAT SHIP WHICH IS SAID TO HAVE BEEN ALTERED CONSIDERABLY BECAUSE SHE ROLLED TOO MUCH: THE GREAT HAMBURG-AMERIKA LINER "IMPERATOR" AT THE NEW AMERIKA PIER AT CUXHAVEN.

The British press were not shy in reporting how modifications had been necessary to improve *Imperator*'s seagoing qualities over the course of her 1913–14 refit. She made the first crossing of her second season in March 1914. (*Illustrated London News*, 1914/Author's collection)

Boat Drill on the Steamship "IMPERATOR", the largest vessel afloat. This mammoth ship carries 83 large life boats and two high powered motor boats, the later equipped with wireless telegraphy. All of them can be lowered by special cranes from either side of the boat in a few seconds and have a capacity of over 5,000 persons.

Britannic was the largest and most luxurious of the White Star Line's three 'Olympic'-class ships. Unlike her older sisters *Olympic* and *Titanic*, she was never the largest liner in the world, but she had the distinction of being the largest British liner by gross tonnage. (Author's collection)

This period postcard highlights a pre-war boat drill on *Imperator*. Cunard's naval architect, Leonard Peskett, took an interest in her lifeboat arrangements. He noted: 'All the boats are manipulated by Welin's davits, those amidships being worked by electrical power. All the lifeboats are built of oak ... The Engelhardt boats are also built of oak (clincher) and in most instances are stowed in groups of three without any immediate supports. This system is not allowed by the British Board of Trade.' The number of lifeboats necessitated having twenty of them over the forecastle deck, eighteen 'on top of boat deck house', twelve on C-deck and twelve on A-deck. (Author's collection)

Although HAPAG's gross profit rose over 29 per cent from 1911 to 1912 and the company increased its dividend, expenses rose by 20 per cent. The company had raised money by issuing more shares to investors. Unfortunately, '*Imperator*, on its first season, suffered a loss of 103,000 marks, excluding its share of the company's overheads (an estimated 380,000 marks).'[4] Construction costs had eventually reached 39 million marks rather than the estimated 25 million marks. Johannes Merck, Ballin's financial director, made calculations that demonstrated 'convincingly that even in the best years these ships were too large and too expensive to generate positive earnings'.[5] Merck felt that the company was heading for 'great difficulties' and that Ballin was overextending himself.[6]

Vaterland created a 'sensation among British shipping in the Solent', when she called at Southampton on 15 May 1914: 'Her progress down the English Channel was as slow and stately as an imperial procession.' The press reported that she had made up to 22 knots 'but she gave the impression at times that she could have leaped into an easy stride of more than 26 knots, which she attained during her trials'. She 'lay for a couple of hours' while tenders took off passengers disembarking and ferried out those joining her for Cherbourg or New York. Speaking to a *New York Times* correspondent, one of the HAPAG directors argued that 'the development of German shipping was, in the view of the Kaiser, one of the great factors for the world's peace'. Once again, Alexander Carlisle was on board. He said she was 'perfect in my opinion. All details have been well arranged and carried out. I consider the steamer is a credit to her builders and owners alike … Germany has now nothing to learn as regards construction of ships and propelling power.' By the time she arrived in New York, she could report an average speed of 23.02 knots and the highest day's run as 592 miles.

In a press interview, Dr Ernst Foerster, 'naval architect of the Hamburg-American Line and the designer of the hull and steel work of the *Vaterland*', said he thought that 'we builders of ships have reached the limit of size for the present time, but this limit is because of the shallowness of water at the entrances to American and European harbours; it is not the limit in possible size of ships nor in engine power nor in naval architecture …' He noted that the ship's subdivision into watertight compartments was regulated by the German authorities but they had exceeded regulatory requirements: 'Ten bulkheads are carried one deck higher than prescribed, and three go two decks higher than is necessary under the rules …' The rudder was 'the largest rudder ever made. It is a balance rudder of 410 square feet and is turned by an engine of 300 horsepower.' Then there were the steam turbine engines, which had developed 63,000 horsepower during the maiden voyage: 'She will attain an average under service conditions of 70,000 or 75,000. On her trial trip the engines developed 90,700 horsepower for four hours, the speed being 25.84 knots.'

Cunard's *Aquitania* made her maiden voyage shortly afterwards, arriving in New York early in June 1914. Meanwhile, White Star's *Britannic* was outfitting at Belfast and NDL had new ships on the way. The competition was relentless.

2

BUILDING A GIANTESS

Shortly after *Vaterland*'s launch in April 1913, preparations were already under way to lay down *Bismarck*'s keel as Blohm & Voss' Yard Number 214. As the third ship, her design benefited from all her owners' and builders' experience operating and building her two older running mates. She was a refined and improved version of both. Years later, Dr Foerster recalled to the *New York Times* that: 'It was the intention to make the *Majestic* the same size as …

the *Vaterland*. The English then were building the *Aquitania*, and the report was that this new ship would be five feet longer than the *Vaterland*. My instructions were then changed to make the *Majestic*, then the *Bismarck*, six feet longer than the *Vaterland*.' In fact, *Aquitania* was never intended to be longer than her German rival. The additional 6ft was 'costly': 'It virtually called for a complete change in plans to add those six feet.'

An early illustration on a postcard of *Imperator* was intended to convey size and strength. Germany was already using the Metric system, whereas Britain continued to work using Imperial measures. (Author's collection)

Imperator's impressive first-class staircase: 'The general treatment is Louis XVI, but the German influence is very apparent.' Again, Cunard were looking at their German rivals while *Aquitania* was under construction. Peskett wrote: 'This portion of the vessel closely resembles the *Aquitania* both in planning and in style of decoration (but the dimensions are smaller) except that the scheme for the *Aquitania* seems much more effective and architectural.' (Author's collection)

'STAGES IN CONSTRUCTION OF THE THIRD VESSEL OF THE *"IMPERATOR"* CLASS ... LAYING THE KEEL OF THE HAMBURG-AMERIKA LINE'S NEWEST AND BIGGEST VESSEL', APRIL 1913

The workmen near the ladder at the bottom left of the image provide a sense of scale. (*Shipbuilding & Shipping Record*, 1914/Author's collection)

Bottom row, left to right:
'Double bottom', 29 May 1913. The double bottom provided very important benefits. It was a strong cellular structure that formed the bottom of the ship's hull, providing strength to the hull and watertight protection in the event that the ship ran aground. The space was not wasted, because the double bottom included tanks that could carry 1,658 tons of fresh water; 2,285 tons of salt water; and 2,157 tons of 'fresh or salt water'. (*Shipbuilding & Shipping Record*, 1914/Author's collection)

'Top of tanks', 26 June 1913. The tank top plating in the engine and boiler rooms included plating 62in wide on the ship's centreline. Elsewhere, it was typically 74¼in wide and ¾in thick, narrowing to 6/10in in thickness near the ship's side and the turn of the bilge. (*Shipbuilding & Shipping Record*, 1914/Author's collection)

'Framing aft, showing propeller struts', 22 September 1913. (*Shipbuilding & Shipping Record*, 1914/Author's collection)

Top row, left to right:
'Frames and decks in course of construction, looking forward', 22 October 1913. The hull frames were just over 11¾in deep and spaced 36in apart amidships. Heavier web frames 33½in deep provided additional structural strength. (*Shipbuilding & Shipping Record*, 1914/ Author's collection)

'View of upper deck looking aft', 13 February 1914. (*Shipbuilding & Shipping Record*, 1914/Author's collection)

'Promenade deck in course of construction', 23 March 1914. (*Shipbuilding & Shipping Record*, 1914/Author's collection)

'Framing (looking forward) of the Hamburg-Amerika Line's Biggest Vessel', 2 December 1913. The beams supporting the decks were 10⅛in deep on the lower decks, decreasing to 9⅘in deep in the case of the beams supporting the 'top deck amidships'. The structural design also included four rows of pillars supporting the decks across the breadth of the ship, spaced on alternative frames. (*Shipbuilding & Shipping Record*, 1914/Author's collection)

Comparing *Bismarck* to *Imperator*, her length between perpendiculars (at the waterline) increased from 882.9ft to 915.5ft; her breadth from 98.3ft to 100.15ft; and her depth from 57.1ft to 58.2ft. Her gross tonnage (a measure of the total enclosed space) rose from 52,117 to 56,551 tons compared to her older running mate. Not only was *Bismarck* going to be longer and larger, but her hull showed the same improvements incorporated into *Vaterland*'s design. *Imperator*'s elliptical or counter stern was a relatively traditional arrangement similar to the White Star liner *Olympic*'s, with the rudder partially submerged and the upper section above the waterline. *Vaterland*'s stern was different. *Scientific American* noted in May 1914:

As compared with the *Imperator* … *Vaterland*, to the eye of any but the expert, looks to be practically identical, her increase in length of 41 feet being scarcely perceptible on a ship of such great dimensions. Her underwater form, however, and the construction of the hull at the stern are quite different, the *Vaterland* having what is known as a cruiser stern, with a balanced rudder which is entirely below the waterline. The form of the *Vaterland* also differs greatly from that of the *Imperator*, the successive water planes aft being fuller than those of the earlier ship. We understand that the changes in her model, as compared with the *Imperator*, had much to do with the high speed which she achieved on her [sea] trial.[1]

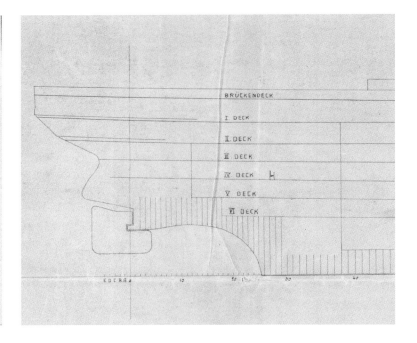

An English language HAPAG advert from June 1914 listed the company's global services. Their London office was on the same road as White Star's: Cockspur Street. (Author's collection)

Vaterland's and *Bismarck*'s stern design was more efficient and modern than that of their older running mate *Imperator*. The rudder (seen at the left) was entirely submerged, whereas much of *Imperator*'s was above the water. (This is *Bismarck*'s stern seen on a plan produced by Blohm & Voss.)(United Kingdom National Archives)

Imperator shortly after she entered service. The reverse reads: 'Nr. 18 Southampton verlassend' (leaving Southampton). (Author's collection)

Dr Foerster attributed a saving of about 2,000hp to the improved rudder design and a saving of 2,000hp to operating with a deeper draft at the stern. The designs of *Vaterland* and *Bismarck* both adopted the same features. Their builders made several models and ran tests in two different test tanks. (In July 1922, *Scientific American* claimed substantially higher savings. They reported the improvement was 'largely' due to the cruiser stern: 'The design of the ship called for the

development of between 15,000 and 16,000hp on each of [the] four lines of [propeller] shafting, and it was estimated that with 63,000hp the ship would show a speed of about 23½ knots'. Foerster thought a cruiser stern gave 'ample space, increased stability, less vibration, and higher efficiency of propellers'.) Despite these advances, *Vaterland* needed plenty of coal. She had bunkered about 8,700 tons on departure from Cuxhaven and burned about 8,200 tons over

3,762 miles from Cuxhaven to Sandy Hook (coming into New York). It all amounted to a consumption of somewhat under 1,200 tons of coal every twenty-four hours.[2] Both ships were slightly wider than *Imperator*, contributing to their stability and passenger comfort at sea.

Even with these improvements, the simple reality was that *Bismarck*'s enormous size required propelling machinery significantly more powerful than that of the record-breaking *Mauretania*, merely to achieve a speed several knots slower. Two additional boilers were needed in the foremost boiler room, taking the total number from forty-six to forty-eight (twelve in each of the four boiler rooms). In December 1913, the *Scientific American* noted the results of calculations made while *Imperator* was being designed. The designers had considered what was necessary to raise her speed from 23 to 26 knots 'and it was found that at least two of the upper decks would have to be sacrificed; that the hull would have to be fined out until the displacement and therefore the carrying capacity had been greatly reduced, and that the increase in motive power, coupled with this reduction in passenger-carrying capacity, would render the ship an … unprofitable venture'. *Bismarck*'s propelling machinery alone occupied 46 per cent of the ship's enclosed space and it weighed over 8,200 tons. Compared to Cunard's smaller *Aquitania*, which was designed for a similar speed, *Bismarck*'s machinery required 26 per cent more space in absolute terms: space that could not be used for revenue-earning purposes such as accommodating passengers or storing cargo. Despite that, she had 13.5 per cent more space available than *Imperator* to use for passengers and cargo and almost 20 per cent more than *Aquitania*, because she was so much larger.

Blohm & Voss wanted to make sure that they could take full advantage of the ship's size to arrange the passenger accommodation, particularly the first-class public rooms. Traditionally, the boiler uptakes in the middle of passenger liners rose straight up the middle of the ship from the boiler rooms to the funnels and detracted from the layout of the accommodation, which had to be arranged around them. *Vaterland* and *Bismarck* had a new arrangement. They split them into two separate uptakes so that one was towards the port side and one towards the starboard side. Dr Foerster described the 'truly unique feature': 'each funnel, instead of rising through the centre of the ship, as is the case in other vessels, rises in two branches, one on each side of the boat, these branches only meeting above the sun deck to form the funnel as seen from the outside'. 'From the new arrangement … there is possible a perspective of more than 300 feet, including the ballroom, the main vestibule, what is called "the tunnel" between the divided hatches, the winter garden and the Ritz-Carlton restaurant. This affords a vista of a kind which has never been seen before on shipboard …'

Their plans included the first-class *Rauchsalon* (smoke room) forward on the *Bootsdeck* (boat deck/A-deck); *Damensalon* (ladies' room) forward, then the two-deck-high *Halle* (lounge), Wintergarden (palm court) and Ritz-Carlton restaurant amidships; and Bridge room aft on the *Oberes Promenadendeck* (upper promenade deck/B-deck). The prime first-class suite and staterooms were on the *Unteres Promenadendeck* (lower promenade deck/C-deck), including the two *Kaiserzimmer* ('Imperial') suites. Second-class public rooms were aft on the *Brückendeck* (bridge deck/D-deck), including a *Rauchzimmer* (smoke room), *Turnhalle* (gymnasium), *Schreibzimmer* (writing room) and *Gesellschaftszimmer* (lounge). Third-class public rooms aft on the same deck included a *Damensalon* (ladies' room) and *Rauchsalon* (smoke room). On I deck (E-deck), fourth-class passengers had an enclosed promenade area forward and third-class a *Speisesall* (dining room) with 363 seats aft. On II deck (F-deck) forward, fourth-class passengers had a *Rauchzimmer* (smoke room) on the port side and a *Damensalon* (ladies' room) on the starboard side, followed by a *Speiseraum* (dining room) with 363 seats; the upper part of the huge first-class swimming pool and the first-class *Speisesall* (dining saloon) with 650 seats were amidships; and the second-class dining saloon with 360 seats aft. (*Bismarck*'s plans anticipated accommodation for about 1,060 first-, 545 second- and 2,392 third- and fourth-class passengers.)

First-class accommodation would be lavish and largely identical to *Vaterland*'s. An old joke was that HAPAG (an abbreviation for Hamburg-Amerikanische Packetfahrt-Actien-Gesellschaft) actually stood for 'Haben Alle Passagiere Auch Geld?', a question asking whether the passengers had plenty of money. First-class staterooms would all have brass bedsteads with no upper berths at all. The specifications included a marble washstand with fresh hot and cold running water and plenty of practical comforts such as twin outlets for electric plugs. *Vaterland* herself had 136 staterooms 'with private bath and toilet or shower and toilet, almost unheard-of luxuries', while the double rooms were an average of 172 sq ft (compared to an average of 43 sq ft on a HAPAG ship in 1886). The public rooms on the upper decks were on a magnificent scale with the first-class dining saloon advertised as the largest afloat. The swimming pool with its Roman décor was a great contrast with its smaller, utilitarian counterparts on board *Olympic* or *Aquitania*. The second-class gymnasium was a welcome innovation and something White Star had also adopted on their new *Britannic*.[3]

Construction progressed rapidly. *Bismarck*'s launch date was set for Saturday, 20 June 1914, about fourteen months after she was laid down and some four months faster than *Vaterland* had taken to get to launch.

Kaiser Wilhelm II and Albert Ballin attended *Bismarck*'s launch. Within weeks, Germany was at war – a war that would end with the Kaiser exiled to the Netherlands and Albert Ballin's death. (*Süddeutsche Zeitung* Photo/ Alamy Stock Photo)

Bismarck's vast hull gathers pace down the slipway ... (Author's collection)

... and safely reaches the water. Her launching weight of about 31,000 tons was almost twice as great as *Lusitania*'s only eight years earlier. (Author's collection)

In Britain, the press covered the launch of the 'world's greatest ship', but with a few paragraphs rather than the extensive coverage they might have devoted to a British liner. The *Daily Mail* thought it was a good sign:

for the success of the new liner that the naming of the latest gigantic addition to the Hamburg-American fleet was performed by a granddaughter of the Iron Chancellor. In performing the ceremony, Countess Hannah von Bismarck said 'By command of his Majesty the Kaiser I name thee *Bismarck*'. When throwing the bottle of wine against the ship's bows the youthful countess failed to use sufficient force, and the bottle did not break. At once, the Kaiser sprang forward, and, seizing the cord by which it was suspended, dashed the bottle into fragments against the ship's steel side, amid the cheers of the spectators.

The Shipbuilder journal noted that her launching weight was about 31,000 tons – a new world record and about 5,000 tons heavier than *Imperator*.[4] It was an impressive accomplishment and Ballin looked forward to her completion the following year. Unfortunately, in a matter of weeks Europe was plunged into the nightmare of the 'Great War'.

Although HAPAG were proud that *Bismarck* would be the largest ship in the world, this period postcard used a photograph of her older, smaller sister *Imperator* to stand in for her. (Author's collection)

Imperator was laid up throughout the conflict and *Bismarck* was incomplete, but their sister *Vaterland* saw more action. She was in New York when the war began. After the United States entered the war, she became a troopship under the name *Leviathan*. During the course of her service, she carried thousands of American troops to Europe and aided the Allies' efforts to defeat Germany. Later on, she brought American troops home and docked at Hoboken, New Jersey, in September 1919. Then she was laid up for several years, pending an extensive refit. (*L'Illustration*, 1919. Classic Image/Alamy Stock Photo)

3

HAMBURG: 'CITY OF SILENCE'

Vaterland arrived in New York on 30 July 1914 and she was still docked at the neutral American port when hostilities broke out. Fortunately, *Imperator* had left New York fourteen days earlier and she returned to Germany safely. Despite the war, some work continued on *Bismarck* at Hamburg. By the early part of 1915, Blohm & Voss had completed work fitting the four great Parsons steam turbine engines on board 'under the most careful supervision' of representatives from HAPAG, the builders and Germanischer Lloyd's. (The turbines were constructed under licence from Charles Parsons' company in Britain and they had provided advice on the installation.) Throughout the war, they took 'the utmost care' of the propelling machinery. Ballin himself wrote in October 1915 of 'the fortunate military situation in which we find ourselves, and which bears all the signs of a further happy and speedy settlement of this cruellest of all wars', but the fighting continued. Later in the war, material such as copper piping was reportedly removed from the ship for war purposes. Unfortunately, she lay afloat for a long period during the conflict and, as a result, the surfaces of many of the double bottom plates became 'very rough' due to 'corrosion that occurred whilst the vessel was lying afloat'. Early in November 1918, Germany was rapidly heading for defeat. A Soldiers' and Workers' Council was established in Hamburg and they occupied HAPAG premises. Albert Ballin did not live to see Germany's surrender. Terry Coleman recorded in *The Liners*:

Ballin swallowed a handful of sleeping tablets, and on November 9th he was dead. His friends disagreed whether it was an accident or suicide, but Ballin himself had said he had no wish to survive to see the Hamburg-Amerika Line destroyed, and Germany vanquished.[1]

The peace terms would be severe for the German merchant fleet, with vessels over 1,600 tons surrendered to the Allies. *Vaterland* herself had been requisitioned for use as a troop ship following the United States' entry into the war, helping to defeat the nation who created her. The British government was keen to replenish the enormous war losses the nation had suffered, including high-profile ships such as Cunard's *Lusitania* in May 1915 and White Star's *Britannic* in November 1916. The Cunard and Anchor Lines had entered the war with twenty-one steamers on North Atlantic routes, adding another five during the conflict. By February 1918, Cunard's chairman was deeply concerned for the future: of those twenty-six steamers, fifteen had been lost, representing 199,573 out of 390,597 gross tons.

Imperator and *Bismarck* were allocated to the United Kingdom. White Star desperately needed to replace *Britannic* on their express service and Cunard had the same need to replace *Lusitania*. Contrary to popular belief, they were not simply allocated specific German ships. They would have to come to an agreement on purchasing them from the British government.

(*Britannic* was lost in service as a hospital ship. White Star had already been paid full compensation in cash by the government.) On 21 July 1920, representatives from the White Star Line, including chairman Harold Sanderson and Arthur B. Cauty, and Harland & Wolff, including Edward Wilding, met with German representatives including Dr Blohm at the Hague, in the Netherlands. Sanderson opened the meeting on the assumption that 'the present negotiations proceeding between the White Star Line and the British government resulted in the vessel being purchased by the White Star Line':

> In this event, it was intended that the ship should be completed for, and run by the White Star Line as one of their own vessels but that, just as in the case of the *Imperator*, the Cunard Co. and the White Star Line would both have a financial interest in the ship. All orders to the builders and all arrangements for completion and the carrying out of any alterations necessary for the new service of the ship would be given by the White Star Line or by their advisers, Messrs. Harland & Wolff.
>
> He pointed out that the White Star Line had no technical staff of their own and were dependent for advice on such matters on their builders and hoped that he could equally rely on Messrs. Blohm & Voss in the same way.
>
> He went on to say that he hoped Mr. Blohm would appreciate the feeling he had, without in any way reflecting on the builders, of some misgivings as to the possibility of the ship being satisfactorily completed in Germany under present conditions and stated that he would like to be assured that there would be no difficulty in this matter either from the firm's staff or their workmen.

Sanderson referred to Blohm & Voss' 'great reputation', saying he was convinced that they would be able to complete the ship in Germany 'to the best of their ability'. Nonetheless, he wanted a representative of Harland & Wolff to be stationed at Hamburg 'to assist in arranging that the ship should be completed in accordance with the standard practices of the new ownership' and report progress. Blohm thanked Sanderson 'for the frank way in which he had explained the situation'. He assured him that Blohm & Voss 'would give the same attention to the work as if she were being completed for a German ownership. He was jealous of their reputation as shipbuilders and would do everything possible to see that the ship was completed in accordance with their traditions and with the requirements of the new owners.' They would give their support to the Harland & Wolff representative. The German government were pressuring the shipbuilder to continue work only 'in accordance with the present design': 'they were giving out no further orders for new material for the ship'.

Nine days later, White Star's Superintendent Engineer W.J. Willett Bruce and the Ministry of Shipping's Mr Boyd inspected the ship. There was a lot of positive news to report alongside particular challenges. The propelling machinery spaces were 'all nearly complete' and Blohm & Voss estimated the work could be completed in six weeks with about three hundred workmen. Her propellers were not yet installed and there was a shortage of bronze, forcing them to use cast steel:

> The steering gear is actually in its compartment ready for sliding into position after the rudder has been shipped. The masts, mast tables, bulwarks, rails, davits, boat control gear, and castings are all in position. Priming coats have been applied to nearly all steel work, and these are in good condition, but no final painting has been done anywhere on the ship. No Navigating Bridge equipment is on board, though it is understood all has been ordered, and the connections are now being completed. The teak wood Charthouse is almost complete.

The passenger accommodation was not so positive:

> In the First Class Public and Luxe Rooms, no decoration has been done. This work is a separate Owners' contract upon which all work has been stopped in view of the uncertainty as to the future of the ship. In general, no internal fittings have been installed in the Cabins, Turkish, Electric, and other Bathrooms; no lifts have as yet been installed. Ventilation throughout the ship is mechanical, and ventilation trunking is generally in place. All main leads for bell wiring and electric light are complete; no fittings are yet installed. In the 2nd Class Dining Saloon, the material is all finished and waiting erection. Nothing is on board for the remaining 2nd Class Public Rooms. 2nd Class Staterooms were all locked up, and the inference is that most of the work is completed. Neither 3rd Class accommodation aft nor 4th Class forward was inspected, but the impression gained was that the spaces were finished, but no fittings in place.

The 'heavy fittings' were all completed in the galleys and pantries but special machinery 'such as dough mixers' was not yet installed. None of the tiles throughout the ship had been laid because of the 'extreme difficulty in obtaining tiles in Germany'. Altogether, she was '85 to 90 per cent completed'. After being told the British authorities were considering completing the ship in the United Kingdom, Dr Blohm said he thought she could be completed in about nine months in Germany, using 2,000 to 2,500 workmen. Edward Wilding thought it would take longer to complete her in the United Kingdom 'as time would be required to pick up the work that had already been done … the determining factor would be the time taken in completing the necessary decorations of the public rooms …'

Early in October 1920, *Bismarck* suffered a fire on board. The *New York Times* quoted a cable sent on 5 October 1920 from Berlin that a fire had broken out during the previous night: 'The cause of the outbreak is not yet known. This morning the interior of the vessel was almost completely burned out.' They even referred to her in the past tense, as if the ship had been destroyed. Shortly afterwards, other reports out of Hamburg referred to 'one room above the engine room' destroyed. At the end of October 1920, the *Liverpool Journal of Commerce* reported a question had been asked in the House of Commons. The government responded that the damage was 'estimated at about £20,000' and that officers from the Reparation Commission had been unable 'to ascertain the cause of the fire'. (Some years later, a Board of Trade official referenced an oil bunker on the starboard side, writing: 'a fire occurred in the bunker before the vessel left the builders'.) There was some suspicion as to the cause of the fire, nonetheless the builders and the German government were responsible for handing her over completed. Any act of sabotage would not have been to Germany's benefit.

In November 1920, Cunard director Sir Percy Bates was concerned about the terms and prices on offer for *Kaiserin Auguste Victoria*, *Imperator* and *Bismarck*. Cunard's Finance Committee were 'ready to regard' them 'as a bargain. Now we are by no means so sure.' Late in October 1920, Chairman Alfred Booth was 'still thinking of the purchase as a bargain', but Bates thought of it as a question 'of how much we are prepared to pay to avoid seeing the ships to go quarters with which we shall find it difficult or uncongenial' to come to a working arrangement with (he cited Furness Withy & Co. among others). If White Star had one of the former HAPAG ships, '*Olympic*, our *Mauretania* and *Aquitania* will do better if the White Star have the *Imperator* as well as the *Olympic*'. Bates opined:

Leave this on one side, personally I consider the *Imperator* no longer as a bargain at the price which we have offered, and while I would not suggest trying to sell the two monsters which we do own, I believe that before very long we shall realise that capital in other forms of ships will be more remunerative. Consequently on this ground alone I would prefer to see the White Star own the *Imperator* … I strongly believe the purchase by them of the *Bismarck* will be either impossible or only possible at an outrageous figure … I would be unwilling to see the White Star running the *Olympic*, *Imperator* and the *Bismarck* if bought at a reasonable [price]. I would prefer to run the *Aquitania* and *Mauretania* against the *Olympic* and *Imperator* rather than run the *Aquitania*, *Mauretania* [and] *Imperator* against the *Olympic* alone.

He was concerned passenger ticket rates would be reduced if one of the monster ships was 'run by itself': 'if the chairman's expectation of rapidly falling prices is realised … this fall must be accompanied by widespread loss of money by the very class on which we are to rely to fill the monsters at the rates which they alone of all passenger ships require'.

On 27 January 1921, Cunard and White Star signed an agreement with the British government. It provided for a joint purchase with a total purchase price of £1.5 million (£500,000 for *Imperator*/*Berengaria* and £1 million for *Bismarck*). Each ship would be bought in ten equal instalments, with interest (at a minimum of 4 per cent) charged on the cost outstanding. Each company would own their ship in its entirety,[2] but pay the other 50 per cent of their ship's profit. On 12 March 1921, Harland & Wolff noted that 'White Star Line have made an offer for her to Lord Inchcape (acting on behalf of the government), which offer has been tentatively accepted.' In April 1921, Cunard's annual report noted that they had purchased *Imperator* and renamed her *Berengaria*. By 16 November 1921, Cunard and White Star had signed an agreement about how they would operate both ships on a joint account.

Below: A plan of *Bismarck* at the tank top level, showing the layout of all the compartments and machinery spaces at the bottom of the ship. She had a total of forty-eight Yarrow water tube boilers (with 240 burners) in the four boiler rooms, working at a pressure of 240lb per square inch. The sheer scale of the propelling machinery is illustrated by the fact that the total heating surface was 219,504 sq ft. Following completion as an oil burner, the main oil bunkers and the oil tanks in the double bottom could accommodate 8,717 tons of oil fuel. She consumed an estimated 840 tons per day (148 tons every 100 nautical miles) at her normal service speed. (Copyright Lionel Codus 2022)

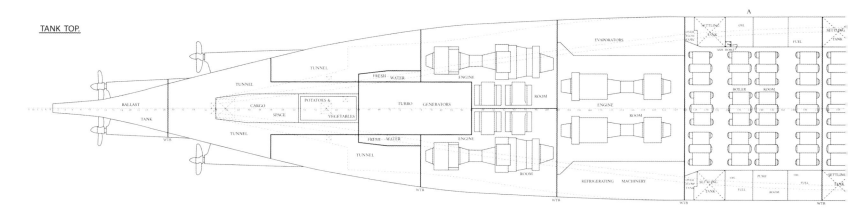

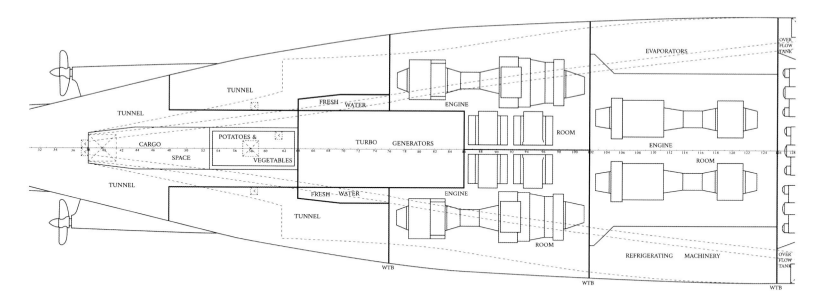

Close-up showing *Bismarck*'s turbine engine and electrical dynamo rooms. She had five dynamos made by Allgemeine, Elec. Ges., Berlin with a total output of 1,440kW. In addition, she had emergency dynamo capacity of 70kW. Throughout the ship were various fresh and salt water tanks (3,815 tons of fresh water and 3,282 tons of salt water). There was a 'grand total' of 38,160 cu ft of ordinary and refrigerated cargo space throughout the ship. (Copyright Lionel Codus 2022)

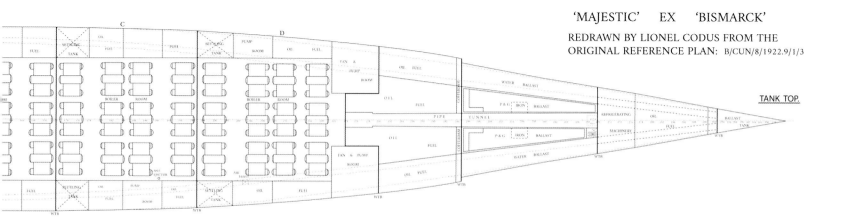

'MAJESTIC'   EX   'BISMARCK'

REDRAWN BY LIONEL CODUS FROM THE
ORIGINAL REFERENCE PLAN: B/CUN/8/1922.9/1/3

TANK TOP.

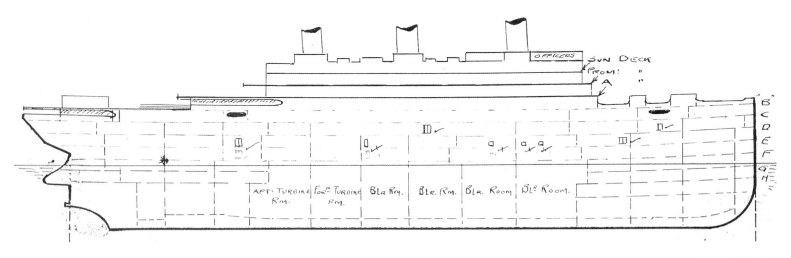

This Board of Trade sketch from 1932 is not drawn to scale; however, it was intended to illustrate the general layout of the transverse watertight bulkheads and the watertight subdivision. The ticks indicate gangway doors in the ship's side and the ticks with a cross through them indicate oiling doors. *Majestic*'s thirteen transverse watertight bulkheads divided her hull into fourteen watertight compartments, meaning that each compartment represented about 7.1 per cent of her waterline length. By comparison, the average length of a watertight compartment on earlier liners such as *Mauretania* (1907) and *Olympic* (1911) was proportionally smaller: 5.9 and 6.2 per cent respectively. (The deck designations follow the post-1929 nomenclature – see page 84)(United Kingdom National Archives)

Two of *Majestic*'s propellers, from a postcard dated 5 September 1928. In July 1920, Edward Wilding had reported that the ship's propellers were 'being made of cast steel, in view of the shortage of bronze'. *Majestic*'s original propellers were replaced by a new set in November 1922 and she went through a number of different ones during her career. Oddly enough, the ship was described as merely the 'largest Atlantic liner' even though she was the largest liner in the world. The reverse reads: 'Casting Weight 30 tons each; Finished weight 15¼ tons each; Diameter 16½ feet; Revolving at 200rpm; Each transmitting approx. 20,000shp, made of STONE's Turbiston Bronze.' (Author's collection)

Despite press speculation in February 1921, when White Star officials were quoted as saying *Bismarck* would be renamed *Oceanic*, the company decided to name her *Majestic*. The term was certainly being used in official correspondence in March 1921. That month, Harland & Wolff advised the Board of Trade that all structural work was complete, with the ship's machinery 95 per cent finished. The key was now outfitting the passenger accommodation. It would take about twelve months. They wanted guidance from the British authorities to make sure she could be granted a passenger certificate under British regulations. The Board suggested improvements to the watertight subdivision. The Convention rules would require 'a three compartment standard throughout' so that the ship could remain afloat with any three watertight compartments flooded; and 'the floodable length at the fore end should be at least 28 per cent of the vessel's length and should consist of at least four compartments'. Unfortunately, if the ship was assigned a draft of 38ft 6in as intended, it appeared 'these conditions are only partially attained'. The floodable length at the bow accounted for about 25 per cent of her overall length. (*Olympic*'s was about 36 per cent.) Further aft 'a good two compartment standard is attained and probably a three compartment standard' abaft the aft watertight bulkhead in the main engine room. They noted that if the watertight bulkhead on frame 197 (the aft bulkhead in the forward boiler room) was extended to D-deck then there would be a three-compartment standard 'forward of that'; and if the watertight bulkhead on frame 172 (the aft bulkhead of the second boiler room) was extended to E-deck then there would be a three-compartment standard 'for about 44 per cent of the vessel's length' forward of that and probably the same further aft. Two other watertight bulkheads could 'probably' not be extended to E-deck because the first-class dining saloon was in the way. The sanitary discharges through the ship's sides were 'not equal to those required' by the Board of Trade but 'they appear to be … efficient and might … be accepted in the circumstances'. Two hinged watertight doors on G-deck 'should be replaced by doors of the sliding type'. The Board noted they needed to consider 'the effect of flooding the large longitudinal side bunkers' under the 'Instructions Relating to the Construction of Passenger Steamships'. (Their approximate calculations suggested that, if all the oil fuel bunkers abreast number 3 boiler room were flooded then the ship would list more than 7 degrees. Under the instructions, if the ship's list 'would render it difficult to utilise all the vessel's boats … arrangements must be fitted for counteracting the list …') Then there was means of access from third-class accommodation on the lower decks. Above G-deck, the width of the staircases needed to be increased. In the event, not all the suggestions proved necessary.

Then there was the question of lifeboats. The Board of Trade's Principal Ship Surveyor E.W. Colvill said that 'the number of sets of davits' to lower and raise the boats 'complies with the rules', but he acknowledged that the 'number of persons' capacity of the German-built lifeboats might not be as high under the British rules. On 25 April 1921, he noted the German plans Edward Wilding had supplied made provision for '36 sets of davits or 34 launching stations' and '42 class I boats, 2 motor boats, and 23 class II boats' whose estimated total capacity was 'sufficient to comply' with the rules. The arrangement was similar to *Berengaria*'s. The deck plans showed 3,818 passengers 'and a crew of about 1,148, making a total of 4,966' passengers and crew. The plans were generally satisfactory but he was concerned that 'if the boats on the after boat deck at the time of launching will be brought into dangerous proximity to the aftermost propellers, as seems probable, they will require to be moved into other positions, as for instance to [the] after end of promenade deck'. He wrote that 'if boat accommodation cannot be provided for the total number of passengers and crew, approved life rafts may be carried in lieu of boats …' Early in July 1921, a surveyor filed a report of a visit to 'the village of Motzen (on the Weser below Vegesack) in connection with the lifeboats of the *Westminster Abbey*'. He 'took the opportunity to inspect the largest type of the boats for the *Majestic*' at the Hinr. Oltmann Bootswerft. They were 30.7ft long, 10.1ft in breadth and 4.1ft deep with oak keels. He found that the 'materials and workmanship are of best quality' but suggested some changes including adding 'yellow metal buoyancy tanks'. By October 1921, plans for stowing *Majestic*'s lifeboats had been submitted to the Board. The plans showed a total of sixty-four boats with a capacity of 4,280 people, using Simpson's rule to convert their cubic capacity into 'persons':

Number of lifeboats	Capacity	Total capacity
18	78	1,404 people
12	67	804 people
6	44	264 people
2	22	44 people
24 collapsible	70	1,680 people
2 motor boats	42	84 people
Totals: 64		4,280 people

The estimated total number of passengers and crew was now reduced to 4,923 but the lifeboat capacity fell short and amounted to about 87 per cent of *Majestic*'s maximum number of passengers and crew. There was 'little likelihood that a larger number of persons' than the lifeboat capacity 'will be carried at least for a considerable time'. Senior Nautical Surveyor J.B. Pope inspected the ship with officials including White Star's marine superintendents, Captain Bartlett and Captain Steel. He was 'satisfied that the proposed arrangements are the best that can be made with the least possible cost'. Compared to earlier plans, some inside boats forward had been removed; two sets of davits were increased in size 'to take a full size class 1A lifeboat with a motorboat over'; and transporter gear and four additional boats were to be fitted at the stern 'so that ten out of the twelve boats may be put out on either side of the ship'.

Edward Wilding had 'understood that [all] these [German] vessels, which are in many respects almost completed from pre-war times, are to be regarded as favourably and as leniently as possible by the Board of Trade surveyors, provided that the requirements of the official German classification and certifying authorities are fully met'. He was worried some officials 'are raising a number of points somewhat unnecessarily', arguing on 24 August 1921: 'I do wish to put it forward that, where good continental practice and experience has provided a substitute equivalent to the usual English practice and experience, it should be regarded as favourably as possible without the letter of English regulations being insisted upon.'

The Board's officials took a pragmatic approach in a number of cases, including suggesting in November 1921 that the two hinged watertight doors on G-deck did not need replacing with sliding doors, provided that the surveyor was satisfied the number of hinged watertight doors were the 'minimum compatible with the efficient working of the ship'. On 10 October 1921, the White Star Line Committee at Hamburg raised the issue of her turbines with the Board of Trade's surveyor, Thomas Miller. The Board of Trade wanted the turbines opened up for inspection but they begged 'to ask you to refrain from pressing this point'. Blohm & Voss and the German government were satisfied and 'steaming trials will be made entirely at their risk'. Opening them up for inspection and then closing them would take a long time 'during which they would be exposed to sabotage': 'The risk of sabotage in this port is real.' The builders refused to even consider it and 'decline to remove even a manhole door'. The Board conceded the point, provided sea trials were satisfactory, but would only issue a passenger certificate for six months. When that expired, they wanted the turbines opened up for inspection. (Another issue was disinterest. The Atlas Werke, Bremen, had installed 'the hydraulic system for working the watertight doors' and had 'no further interest in the matter'. Miller experienced 'great difficulty' in 'obtaining the further designs required'.) Officials spent a lot of time discussing the work of converting her boilers to burn oil instead of coal.

Majestic Sea Trials: Steam Turbine Power Data Ahead, 31 March 1922			
Turbine	Initial Pressure (lbs/sq in)	Revolutions (rpm)	Horsepower (shp)
High pressure	180	184	19,450
Medium pressure	41	187	18,150
Port low pressure	0.5	181	15,200
Starboard low pressure	0.5	185	17,200
			70,000

During her six hours of steaming trials, *Majestic*'s propelling machinery developed 70,000shp running ahead. When the order 'full speed astern' was given to bring her to rest in the water, she had less power available. At that time, the engines were developing 66,900shp ahead. The astern turbines developed 37,170shp, which was impressive in itself but represented only 56 per cent of the power when she had been running ahead.

While *Majestic* was being outfitted, she stood 'high above the water in the yard of Blohm & Voss' and dominated 'the harbour of Hamburg'. She was visible 'for miles around'. In May 1921 the number of workers engaged on the ship was increased from 1,000 to 2,500. One reporter noted: 'Blohm & Voss say that she will be better than the *Vaterland*, as they have learned by experience.' The *New York Times* wrote in November 1921: 'During much of 1920 and the present year a thousand men have been kept busy on her. Her funnels were hoisted into place last May.' On 27 February 1922, the Board of Trade's surveyor reported he had 'fully surveyed' her hull during the months since August 1921. It had been built according to the plans: 'The whole of the shell plating, riveting … were carefully inspected during the month the vessel was in dry dock and the workmanship is of good quality; the material appears to be of standard quality.' He spotted 'some slight pitting [corrosion] in way of the waterline at which the vessel has been floating for the past eight years … but it is of no consequence from a strength point of view'.

White Star's plans for their express service from Southampton to New York were finally coming together. Since emerging from her post-war refit and conversion to oil fuel in June 1920, *Olympic* had been running well and *Adriatic* partnered her on a temporary service. Now, with *Homeric*'s maiden voyage in February 1922, it was only a matter of months before *Majestic* would complete the trio.

They were an odd assortment in many ways. Only _Olympic_ was serving her original owners (and without her two ill-fated sister ships). _Homeric_'s speed was rather slow for an 'express' service and she was significantly smaller than her running mates. Cunard, who moved their express service to Southampton after the war, had a rather more balanced service with _Mauretania_, _Aquitania_ and _Berengaria_. By gross tonnage, _Mauretania_ was actually smaller than _Homeric_, but their three ships were much closer together in speed and general design. Nonetheless, White Star were undoubtedly pleased they had _Majestic_. They looked forward to taking delivery of the largest liner in the world.

'TOURING _MAJESTIC_'

FIRST CLASS

First-Class Smoke Room
Majestic's first-class smoke room was about 55ft by 55ft in length and width, situated at the fore end of A-deck beneath the bridge. The furniture included brown and green leather settees. (Author's collection)

'Before the big smoking room fireplace': a steward serves a first-class gentleman, in one of many publicity shots used by the White Star Line in the 1920s. (Author's collection)

'A great hall of the Tudor period is suggested by the *Majestic*'s smoking room. Crusaders in chain mail flank the tall stone fireplace. Rafters, pillars and panelled walls are of well-carved oak. On a richly wrought frieze are fixed the arms of the Oxford and Cambridge colleges, each shield in its proper colours. Large paintings adorn the side walls. The front windows give a clear view of the sea ahead – for the room is the choicest location on the ship for observation.' (Author's collection)

Gymnasium
Majestic had two gymnasiums on board, one for first class and one for second class. They were well equipped and offered plenty for those who found regular walks around the ship's decks was not enough exercise. (Author's collection)

Reading and Writing Room
Majestic's reading and writing room:
'... combining the quiet of a library with the elegance of a drawing room. Its windows admit a wealth of daylight, softly diffused through light curtains; while at night the interior of old ivory and Wedgwood blue is softly illuminated by frosted ceiling lights and tall standard lamps with hooded blue silk shades. The room is much favoured by passengers seeking more seclusion than is found in the lounge or palm court.' The carpeting was in blue and grey. (Author's collection)

Photos: First-class passengers had comfortable writing desks to engage in correspondence (top), but there were plenty of comfortable chairs to relax in as well (bottom). The reading and writing room might have been considered largely a ladies' preserve in earlier decades, but gentlemen were able to use it as well. As the 1920s wore on, passengers mixed more than they might have done before the war. The bookcase was carved mahogany in three sections, totalling 21ft 6in long and reaching a height of 10ft in the centre. (Author's collection)

Below: The reading and writing room layout as shown on a 1933 accommodation plan. (Author's collection)

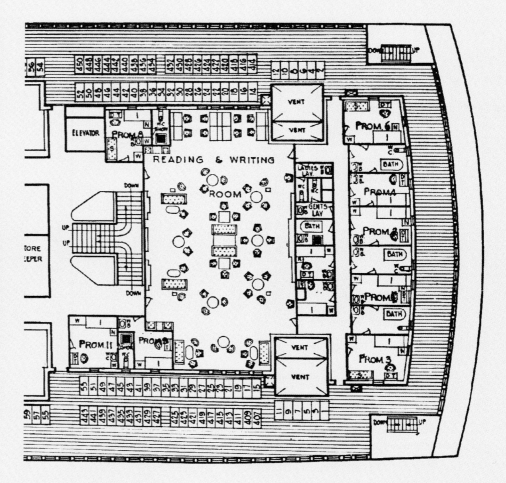

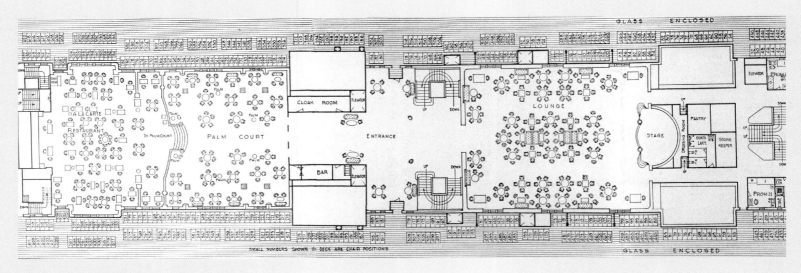

First Class Entrance and Lounge
The vast expanse of B-deck amidships, made possible by the split design of the funnel uptakes, was used to great effect. (Author's collection)

The first-class entrance amidships on B-deck, looking aft and towards the port side. From the left, the doors lead through to the palm court, aft; then, moving to the right, we see the light-coloured door to the large cloakroom; the lift door round the corner; the entrance vestibule leading to the promenade outside (presumably panelled in white enamel as with others on the deck above); and the port side staircase. To the right, out of view, is the first-class lounge entrance … (Author's collection)

… seen here, looking directly ahead into the first-class lounge. (Ioannis Georgiou collection)

Top left: Looking aft and to starboard, through the entrance doors at the aft end of the first-class lounge and into the first-class entrance. (Johnstone White, White Star Memories collection)

Bottom left and right: 'Lofty, spacious, dignified, the *Majestic*'s lounge is distinguished by its perfect symmetry, unbroken by bays, projections or roof supports; by the substantial beauty of its oak-panelled walls with their hand carved ornamentation; by its tall French windows admitting floods of sunshine; by the richness of its ceiling of crystal and carved wood, in which concealed lights at night throw the florid dark carving into bold relief, striking a key note of beauty.' (Author's collection)

Above and right: A closer look at the raised stage at the front of the first-class lounge (Ioannis Georgiou collection) and the 'grand piano of exceptional size and beauty' shown in White Star Line publicity. The grand piano was in oak, by Steinway and Sons. (Author's collection)

First Class Palm Court
Looking forward, from the palm court to the first-class entrance. (Author's collection)

'When in the palm court of the *Majestic* – the Rialto where the ship's world of fashion passes in review – one can scarcely conceive oneself to be afloat. Great palms, tall Corinthian columns, broad windows softly curtained in muslin and cluny, a carpeted promenade, furniture like that of a country club piazza, make the setting perfect to complete the illusion of being on shore. After dinner coffee is served here both to patrons of the main dining saloon and the restaurant.' (Author's collection)

Looking aft, towards the first-class restaurant. (Author's collection)

À La Carte Restaurant

'Design, finish and furnishings in the *à la carte* restaurant on the *Majestic* make it truly an exquisite room. The style is Empire, and the woodwork cedar mahogany, showing under dull finish its perfect grain, lovingly brought out by the art of the craftsman. Small tables are provided for two, four or six persons. The tall windows that admit generous light, are hung with rose silk draperies. The carpet is rose and olive.' The panelling included gold-leafed frieze and figured panels. There were 'six massive fluted centre columns, with scroll tops'. (Author's collection)

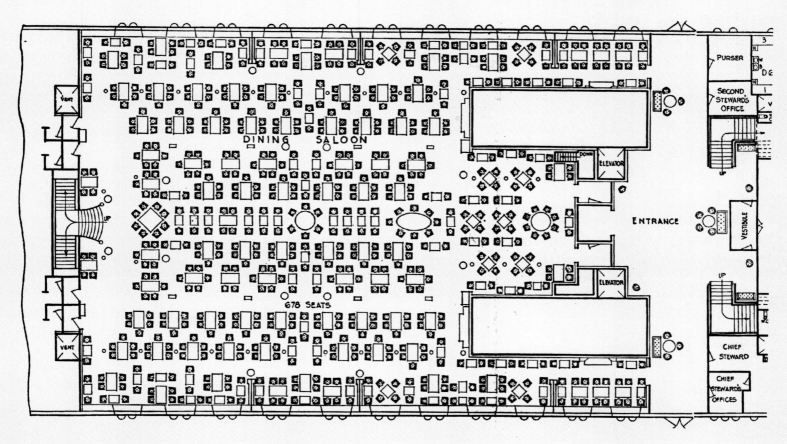

First-Class Dining Saloon

The enormous first-class dining saloon on F-deck: 'Height, airiness, freshness; ample room for superior service, with many small tables; tall windows hung in rose silk, lending its colour warmth to gleaming crystal and silver, snowy napery and white walls – these are features of *Majestic*'s splendid first cabin dining saloon. Outstanding is its lofty central part – with the highest ceiling in a ship – its frescoed dome springing from slim Ionic pillars. The room seats 654 persons and occupies parts of E and F decks.' According to German plans dated October 1921, there were 650 seats. After *Majestic* entered service in 1922, it was reported the saloon could seat 654 people (later increased to 678, as shown on this 1933 accommodation plan). When John Havers toured *Majestic* in January 1936, he recalled the saloon 'with reddish furniture and table lights, cream columns, green railings between the columns on the deck above, where the orchestra played, made this one of the finest rooms I have seen afloat. Perhaps surpassed by the sheer grandeur of the *Normandie* but much more dignified ...' (Author's collection)

Above and right: Two views of the saloon looking forward, from the centre (above) and off to the port side (right). Oddly enough, one of the ceiling lights is not on! (Author's collection)

At the aft end of the saloon was a small staircase. (Author's collection)

White Star publicity showcased the individual tables and the electric lamps. (Author's collection)

First-Class Swimming Pool, Turkish and Electric Baths
'The luxury of Imperial Rome lives again in the swimming bath of the *Majestic*. Decorated in the Pompeian style, with rich marbles and brilliant red mosaics, it is a perfect replica of an ancient bath, plus every modern comfort. Warmed sea water fills it. Turkish and electric ray baths are connected with it. Rubbers, hairdressers, manicures and pedicures are in attendance for both sexes. The tiled pool has an area of 820 square feet and a depth of from three to nine feet.' The swimming pools on *Majestic* and her older sisters still rank among the grandest of any liner and marked a huge advance at the time, compared to the utilitarian facilities on earlier ships such as Cunard's *Aquitania* or White Star's *Olympic* and *Titanic*. (Author's collection)

Ladies pose for a publicity photo. (Author's collection)

The lower level of *Majestic*'s first-class swimming pool, shown on a 1933 accommodation plan. At the top left (on the port side) is the foot bath and many dressing rooms; to the right, is the rest room and electric bath establishment with footbath and spray showers. Directly above these facilities was a gentleman's barber shop and a ladies' hairdressing room. (Author's collection)

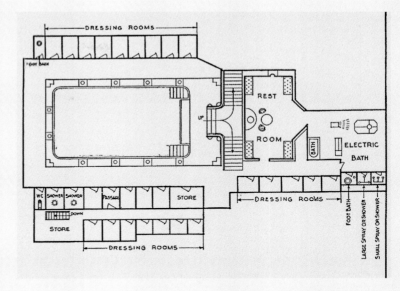

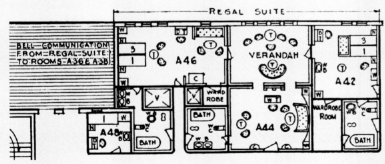

In 1913, Cunard's Leonard Peskett thought that the two Kaiser (or 'Imperial') suites on *Imperator* 'closely resembled the Regal suites on the *Lusitania*, although the general finish and completeness does not compare with these rooms. The main feature was a private floor covered with rubber tiling walls decorated [in the] Louis XVI manner, painted grey.' He was, perhaps, being a bit uncharitable in making the comparison. The suites were arranged so that they could be divided between two different sets of passengers, with each party having the option of using the verandah. When *Majestic* was completed, White Star opted to use the 'Regal' suite designation. This plan shows the port side suite in 1933 (by which time, C-deck had been renamed A-deck). (Author's collection)

One of the sun verandahs in a Regal suite. (Author's collection)

Left: One of the Regal suite bedrooms looking into the sun verandahs. (Author's collection)

Below: The finest first-class suite rooms were spacious and comfortable. (Author's collection)

Above: 'Drawing room and bedrooms alike in the suites on the *Majestic* are equipped with dressing tables having triple mirrors, at which a woman may dress her hair or give finishing touches to her toilette; capacious chests of drawers and generous full length wardrobes, the latter electric lighted and fitted with forms for hanging clothing. Most bedrooms in suites have a pier glass, for full length views of gowns. The baths also have accessories not usually found on ships.' (Author's collection)

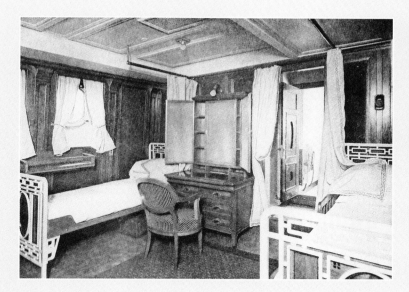 

A two-bed first-class stateroom with connecting private bathroom (left) and 'a typical single bed stateroom' (right). Although *Majestic*'s Regal suites were magnificent and there were other first-class suite rooms on C-deck and D-deck that had interconnecting bedrooms and sitting rooms, she did not have a large number of first-class suites compared to some of her competitors. However, her 'ordinary' staterooms stood out because there were no upper berths, but proper beds; and a very large proportion had private bathroom facilities. (Author's collection)

Majestic had plenty of enclosed and open promenade deck space. (Author's collection)

SECOND CLASS

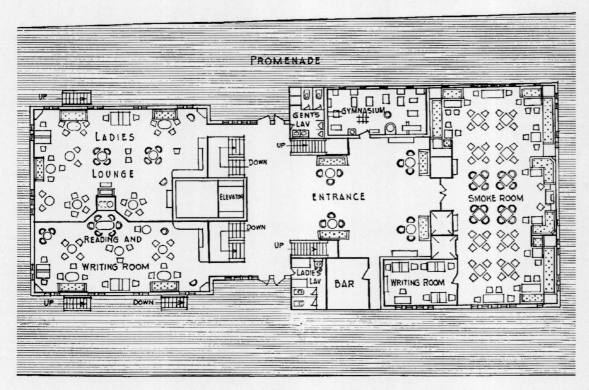

Second-class (later tourist-class) passengers had a wide range of public rooms on *Majestic*. As shown on the plan, a smoke room, writing room, gymnasium, ladies' lounge, reading and writing room, lavatories and a spacious entrance hall were all within a short distance of each other. (Author's collection)

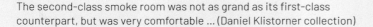

The second-class smoke room was not as grand as its first-class counterpart, but was very comfortable … (Daniel Klistorner collection)

… as was the second-class lounge. (When *Majestic*'s furnishings were being sold in 1936, the lounge contents included '12 round pedestal tables', 47 'Drawing Chippendale Arm Chairs' and 17 'Tub Chairs upholstered in pink moquette'.) (Daniel Klistorner collection)

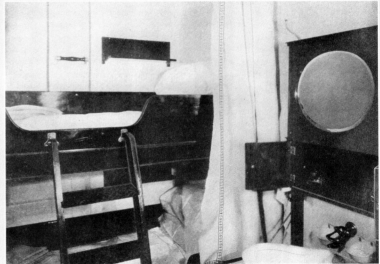

Clockwise from above:
The second-class reading and writing room was comfortable. (Author's collection)

The second-class dining saloon was situated aft on F-deck (seen here prior to the 1928 refit). (Daniel Klistorner collection)

A 'stateroom for two' in second class. White Star publicity said 'second cabin staterooms cause delighted comment'. (Author's collection)

THIRD CLASS

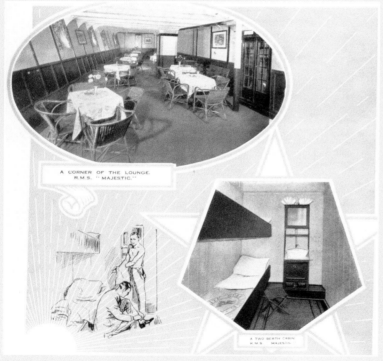

A CORNER OF THE LOUNGE.
R.M.S. "MAJESTIC."

A TWO BERTH CABIN
R.M.S. MAJESTIC

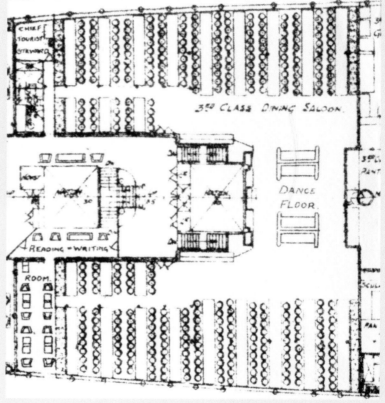

Clockwise from top left:

The third-class dining saloon, aft on E-deck, was somewhat larger than its second-class counterpart. The general arrangement plans published in *The Shipbuilder* in January 1923 stated that it had a capacity of '442 seats'. (The third-class dining saloon forward on F-deck had 363 seats.)(Author's collection)

In later years, there was an area allocated to a dance floor in the middle of the saloon and a reading and writing room was created aft on the starboard side. (Johnstone White, White Star Memories collection)

When *Majestic* entered service, she had a third-class smoke room on the port side and a general room on the starboard side, forward on F-deck (in addition to the larger counterparts aft on D-deck). The curve of the ship's hull is visible as it narrowed towards the bow. In later years, the general room was called a third-class lounge in White Star publicity materials. A two-berth, third-class cabin provided a lot more comfort than third-class accommodation on liners a generation earlier. The vast majority of third-class cabins were two- or four-berth. (see p. 98)(Author's collection)

Above: The third-class smoke room aft on D-deck.
(Ioannis Georgiou collection)

Right: Third-class passengers enjoyed spacious promenade decks, complete with plentiful deckchairs and deck games. (Daniel Klistorner collection)

CREW

Majestic's 'radio room'. (Daniel Klistorner collection)

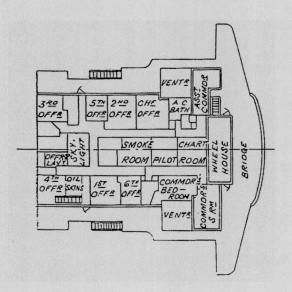

The bridge itself spanned the entire width of the ship. The wheelhouse and chartroom were situated behind the bridge. On the starboard side of the wheelhouse (the bottom right on the plan) is the suite consisting of the commander's sitting room, bedroom and private bathroom; on the port side is the assistant commander's quarters. The other officers' cabins, and smoke room, are also visible. Walnut, oak and maple panelling was used in the fitting out of these rooms and the corridors included white-enamelled softwood panels. The furnishings included 'magnificent mahogany panelling, with two wardrobe doors, 1 cabin door, 1 mirror', which may have formed part of the commander's quarters. (*The Shipbuilder*, 1923/Author's collection)

The newly completed *Majestic* represented an imposing sight as the largest steamer in the world. The bridge looks very dark in this photograph because it retained the original teak. (Author's collection)

4

SWEET SUCCESS

Harold Sanderson, White Star's chairman and managing director, returned from Hamburg in mid-March 1922 with an optimistic view of the ship's future. 'I am very glad to inform you,' he wrote in a letter to Cunard's Sir Thomas Royden, 'that I found the work on her has been proceeding very well indeed, and we have every reason to hope that all will be completed in time for her to leave by the end of this month.' He recorded that *Majestic* 'is really very fine and fully up to all our expectations'. Providing that there were no delays due to high winds or tides, he said:

> … she should leave Cuxhaven for her official trials on March 31st, and thereafter I think we may hope to see her at Southampton by the end of the first week of April, and so she should be able to keep the sailing date for her maiden voyage, as proposed, viz. May 10th.

The White Star Line were eagerly anticipating the *Majestic*'s entry into service and selected a man they held in the highest regard to command her. Towards the end of March 1922, Sir Bertram Hayes – who had left *Olympic* at the beginning of the year – was told to go to Hamburg. An article in the *Southampton Times* reported:

> Captain Hayes has achieved great success on the *Olympic*. He has won the warmest approval of the company; and gained the friendship of thousands of people who have crossed the Atlantic under his care; and he has deservedly earned the respect of every Officer and man who served under him. On his part, he has given unstinted praise to the men who have so loyally served in the *Olympic*, on one occasion describing himself as 'head of a very happy family'. In fair weather and foul, he has been conspicuously skillful in managing the *Olympic*.

Giving him command of the new *Majestic*, the largest vessel in White Star's fleet, was a fitting tribute as his career drew to a close. The reporter continued:

> During his long association with the company Captain Hayes has probably had more honours conferred upon him than any other shipmaster running in the Atlantic trade, not only for saving life at sea, for which he holds medals, cups, and diplomas, but for conspicuous service on many occasions in war and peace.

The White Star Line had dropped the formal commodore title in 1889[1] but decided to restore it, so he became Commodore Sir Bertram Hayes.[2] He found that some of *Majestic*'s officers had established 'more or less friendly relations' with the German workers at Blohm & Voss, even if the foremen and leading hands at the shipyard had been warned

Majestic arrived in Southampton, assisted by tugs. *Olympic's* port side and her first and second funnels are visible ahead *of Majestic's* bow. (She had left New York on 1 April 1922 with 1,462 passengers)(PA Images/Alamy Stock Photo)

not to show too much 'friendliness' to their British colleagues. Mr Harland, one of Harland & Wolff's representatives, and Chief Engineer Joseph Wolff, were both tactful and did much to improve relations. (Rumours that the ship might go to France had been circulating. It was hinted that, if that were the case, she would never leave the Elbe.) When she eventually left Hamburg on the afternoon of 28 March 1922, her German name was on each side of the bow, with '*Bismarck*, Hamburg' on the stern. Her funnels were also painted in the HAPAG colours. The two 'Imperial Suites' were still called 'The Kaiser Suite' and 'The Crown Prince Suite'. The B and C-deck accommodation, for German guests and officials, 'was all in apple pie order' according to Hayes, but his own room on F-deck did not even have a bed. Edward Wilding was one of the few Britishers to enjoy that luxury. 'We were guests [of the German government] no doubt, but it did not appear to us that our hosts had made very strenuous efforts to shine as such,' Hayes wrote.

Majestic's 'official steaming trial of six hours duration' took place on 31 March 1922 in the Heligoland Bight, a bay forming the southern part of the German Bight (near the mouth of the Elbe river). Hayes wrote that 'all the German government required from her builders was that they should produce 66,000 horsepower on the engines': she 'simply steamed for three hours out into the North Sea, and then returned to the same anchorage she had left'. While she was steaming back, 'we asked for a few experiments to be carried out to test her steering and stopping qualities … I must say that she exceeded our expectations in every way she was tried, and, for her size, proved herself to be a very handy ship.' The boiler pressure varied from 220 to 240lb of steam per square inch and her total shaft horsepower (shp) averaged 66,618. During the trial, the maximum power developed was 70,000shp. At that point, her high-pressure turbine was developing 19,450shp at 184 revolutions per minute (rpm). Her propelling machinery was developing 66,900shp when 'the engines were stopped and put full speed astern, bringing the vessel to rest in the water in four minutes from the time the telegraph rang when the vessel was going full speed ahead'.

Following the trials, Blohm & Voss were given another week to complete the outfitting of the passenger accommodation. The British representatives engaged in 'considerable discussion' with the builders, because parts were clearly unfinished. Hayes' complaints were not simply about the accommodation. The food was 'unpalatable': 'raw ham and various kinds of sausage, also raw, formed the staple food for breakfast … most of us could not eat it, we had to content ourselves with the badly cooked porridge that preceded it'. The German 'beer was very good, however, and that with bread and cheese was all that most of us could tackle'. The British contingent used to wind each other up. When someone arrived at the breakfast table, they were 'greeted with mild jokes about certain kinds of food to which we knew they were partial being "off"'. The humour was intended to poke 'fun at each other to keep our spirits up', but some of their German colleagues thought 'we were making jokes about them'.

When it came for the Blohm & Voss representatives to leave, they implored Hayes' crew to 'do the best we could with the ship for the sake of their reputation as her builders'. As soon as they left, workers began to change the ship's name at the bow and stern. The port of registry was changed from Hamburg to Liverpool. Hayes was told that 'Hamburg was referred to as "The City of Silence" when the *Bismarck* left …' *Majestic* left for Southampton at 9 a.m. on 9 April 1922. She had an easy run there. All of her propelling and auxiliary machinery 'worked in a highly satisfactory manner', according to the Board of Trade's Thomas Miller. She arrived flying the British red 'duster' on the morning of 10 April 1922 – ten years to the day that *Titanic* had made her maiden voyage, as the White Star Line's then largest ship and the largest steamer in the world. She was piloted in by the veteran Trinity House pilot, George Bowyer. Hayes had warned him: 'She will be a handful to handle, George.' Bowyer was not put off: '"Well," I thought to myself, "bring along the handful, and let me have a go at her." The time soon came along and I took her in hand, safely docking her for the first time … everybody was pleased and thankful.' Nonetheless, *Majestic*: 'Certainly is a handful, and is quite a different ship from the *Olympic*, and she requires a great deal of watching …' In Hayes' words, 'a strenuous month' was spent preparing the ship for her maiden voyage. On 26 April 1922 the Bill of Sale was completed. Since the ship had now been formally handed over to the White Star Line she was registered in Liverpool at 2 p.m. on 1 May 1922. She was officially the British Board of Trade's ship No. 146,555, with a gross registered tonnage of 56,551.08 tons.

Meanwhile, Southampton had been eagerly awaiting the White Star Line's 'largest ship in the world'. In January 1922 detailed articles were appearing in the local press outlining the new liner's wonders, while there was significant coverage devoted to *Homeric* – running with *Olympic* since February. In an effort to illustrate *Majestic*'s enormous size, a complete list of the ship's stores for her first round trip was published. What a list it was:

75 tons of meat;
10 tons of bacon and hams;
28 tons of fish;
18 tons of poultry;
1,000 each of plover, quail, snipe, grouse, and 500 wild ducks;
30 tons of potatoes;
7 tons of carrots and turnips;
About 10 tons of cabbages;
Several tons of onions and miscellaneous vegetables, including 1,600lb of hot-house tomatoes;

600 boxes of apples;
400 boxes of oranges;
60 boxes of pears;
1 ton of hot-house grapes;
1 ton of ice cream;
3 tons of jams and marmalade;
35 tons of flour;
8 tons of sugar;
5 tons of butter;
3 tons of tea and coffee;
80,000 eggs;
500 gallons of fresh milk;
80,000 bottles of ale and stout;
1,000 quarts and 1,600 pints of champagne;
1,000 quarts and 1,300 pints of other wines;
4,000 bottles of whisky, brandy and gin;
300 bottles of liqueurs;
250,000 cigarettes;
2,240lb of tobacco.

Majestic 'will also carry record quantities of articles of everyday use on board', as a reporter recorded:

45,000 plates;
18,000 spoons;
10,000 forks;
14,000 'weapons of cutlery';
16,500 glasses and tumblers;
27,000 articles of glassware and crystal;
80,000 cups, saucers, plates, dishes and 'other china and earthenware';
178,000 pieces of linen, including 11,000 blankets;
13,000 pillow slips, 'and a like number' of sheets;
45,000 serviettes;
75,000 towels.

Majestic shared with her sister *Leviathan* the distinction of being the most powerful vessel afloat. It was claimed her engines could develop 100,000shp. Yet with all the excitement about the ship's upcoming maiden voyage, there was perhaps a sense of *déjà vu*. She had arrived in Southampton as White Star's latest liner, the largest vessel in the world and the line's new flagship, ten years to the day of *Titanic*'s maiden voyage departure from Southampton. She was to run with *Titanic*'s veteran sister ship *Olympic*, now in her eleventh year of service. The *Southampton Times* reported on 22 April 1922 that *Majestic* was 'a hive of activity as she lies at her berth on Ocean Dock'. They said that 'the blankets alone' weighed 17 tons: 'The bedrooms will be supplied with 8,000 tumblers and 1,600 water bottles.' They reported that there were '3,000 salt, pepper and mustard pots' on board. Some of the quantities of the different items varied according to different press reports, but they were definitely on an enormous scale.

On Wednesday, 3 May 1922, she was open to public inspection. Newspaper reports stated 'over 5,000 people visited the vessel' at a charge of 3 shillings per head in aid of local charities: 'Hundreds went from Bournemouth. It was the first time the *Majestic*, the *Berengaria*, the *Olympic* and the *Mauretania* had been in dock together.' The following Saturday, a number of reporters went over her. 'As we stepped aboard we were taken to the swimming bath full of wonderful-looking sea green water. It was like an ancient Egyptian temple, or Palace, with gorgeous pillars, gorgeous marble fittings, gorgeous floors and dressing rooms', wrote the editor of the *Leicester Evening Mail*. He dubbed her 'a ship of baths': 'There were still the private baths attached to the private suites …' The *Northern Whig*'s reporter wrote there was 'no comparison possible between the crack boat of a quarter of a century ago [White Star's original *Majestic*, completed in 1890] and this, the last word in ship construction, and the largest vessel afloat. *Majestic* she is by name and nature.'

He recalled sailing on Cunard's *Etruria* and *Umbria* in 1908, when they encountered gales and 'plenty of crockery' was smashed, even though they arrived on time. 'No first or any other class of passenger on board of this leviathan will be able to lie awake and listen to the crash of tons of water taken on board over turtle bows dipping into the Atlantic swell … she will ride serenely over the biggest waves, and those on board will be practically unconscious of the nature of the weather …' He did not appreciate the severity of sea conditions on the North Atlantic! He wrote that the 'rudder post, with its plates, totals 140 tons'. The London *Daily News* described her as the 'last word' in safety precautions, noting there were '450 fire alarms and an enormous number of extinguishers'; 'special telephones have been installed in various places, from which messages can be sent to the central bridge from which watch is continually kept …' The 'steel [watertight] bulkheads have been covered with fireproof material, and have fireproof doors, with a temperature resistance of 2,900 Fahrenheit'. They added the 'fireproof and watertight doors' were 'shut or opened by hydraulic control' and noted that two of the lifeboats were motor boats.

The White Star Line hosted the press at a lunch on board, which was covered by the *Belfast News-Letter*. Harold Sanderson explained that 'there is not today in Great Britain a dry dock large enough to accommodate the ship'. He reported that a floating dry dock was on the way 'within the next twelve months'. Arthur Cauty recalled White Star's anxiety as to whether she would sail on time: 'the reason for this was the chaos that ruled in the labour world'. He was careful not to give away any secrets about the ship's speed, but 'he might say that on her trial run from Cuxhaven she developed over 25 knots, and the company felt satisfied she would fulfil all demands and requirements'. The guests were divided into tour groups as they went over the ship. 'The general view was that she certainly represented the climax of passenger ship construction up to the present, and that distinction she is likely to retain for an indefinite length of time, for it appears understood in shipping circles that altered economic conditions since the war will check the production of ships on so mammoth a scale …' Southampton's mayor, Councillor Bath, thanked the White Star Line for opening up *Majestic*. He said local charities would benefit by £600. The only regret was that Lord Pirrie was unable to be with them. He 'had always been a warm friend to the company, for which he had done so much'. The *Southampton Times* wrote about the 'Majestic Pudding': 'Each portion was served in a cup of its own. The basis of the pudding was custard, with a core of apricot. There was a cover of whipped cream in a whorl set off with a preserved cherry and two shreds of angelica, so that the pudding was as pleasing to the eye as it was agreeable to the taste.' The *Northern Whig*'s reporter reflected as they disembarked:

> First and foremost was the regret that it was not the work of Belfast, though it was in some degree consoling to learn that Messrs. Harland & Wolff had played a prominent part in her completion.
>
> One thing that brought home to me her enormous size was that we were actually looking down from the promenade deck of the *Majestic* on the *Mauretania* as she departed for her westward trip. It is not often that one has the opportunity of finding three of the world's great vessels lying within one hundred yards of each other … Not for many years shall we hear of their tonnage being eclipsed …
>
> When one estimates what it would cost today to build such floating palaces one must consider how they can be made to pay. It is evident that the White Star company have arrived at the conclusion that the *Majestic* can be made to pay: but whether, if such a vessel had to be built today, rates could be obtained that would show a profit is a very debatable point …
>
> It seems to me that for many years to come construction will be confined to vessels of medium tonnage, both by reason of the high cost of construction and also because port development is much slower than the growth of ships. He would be a rash individual, however, who would state definitively that we have reached the limit of big construction …

There was a great sense of optimism as *Majestic* began her maiden voyage on 10 May 1922. Newspapers spoke of an enormous crowd watching as the liner glided from her berth. 'Thousands of Southampton people and folk from other towns were present, in addition to those who would in any case have been there to bid goodbye to friends. There was beautiful weather for the spectacle, and a noble one it proved.' On the bridge, Pilot George Bowyer issued the commands for *Majestic* to 'glide slowly from her berth'. Commodore Sir Bertram Hayes' flag flew from the ship. Six tugs assisted the huge liner, and the *Southampton Times* recorded 'the recently dredged enlargement of the swinging ground being called into use [for the departure]'. It was said that 'the vessel was operated with beautiful accuracy, and from the casting off to the shaping for down the river there was no trace of uncertainty'. White Star's Southampton Marine Superintendent Captain Benjamin Steel directed operations from the quay, with Captain Harvey acting as an observer.

She reached Cherbourg and left the French port for New York that evening. The *Journal of Commerce* reported she had made a 'splendid start'. *Majestic* 'was reported 164 miles west of the Lizard at noon yesterday [Thursday, 11 May 1922], her average speed between Cherbourg and the Lizard being over 23 knots. All well and passengers expressing great satisfaction with the ship.' She had on board 655 passengers, including 362 first class, 127 second and 166 third class, which compared to the 705 passengers for *Olympic*'s previous Southampton departure. The party from Harland & Wolff, who were aboard to observe her in service and rectify any minor issues as needed, included Edward Wilding, travelling with his wife Marion, and Henry Harland, who was now married to Thomas Andrews' widow Helen. (Thomas Andrews had lost his life in the *Titanic* disaster a decade earlier. Wilding had then been called upon to give extensive testimony before the Wreck Commissioner's Court about her design and construction.) *Majestic*'s crew included a number of people who had survived that disaster, including George Cavell and George Hogg.

On Monday, 15 May 1922, the *Liverpool Echo* carried a wireless message from *Majestic* at sea: 'We still have good weather; run yesterday, 581 [miles]; today (Sunday) 583; weather permitting, we should be in New York early Tuesday afternoon. Last night had it fairly rough. Ship behaved splendidly.' A 'dutiful son' wrote home to his father from *Majestic* 'near Sandy Hook, Tuesday morning, 16 May 1922'. His letter was reproduced in the *Southampton Times*, representing very favourable publicity for the White Star Line:

Dear Dad,

The *Majestic* has travelled so fast coming out that they say we will catch the Cunarder going home today; thus you will get this in 12 days after we left you at Southampton. Some surprise for you. On the first day out from Cherbourg, eight hours' fog delayed us – hard luck. The ship's big open-sea runs were 594, 581, 583 and 595 miles. Fine indeed for a maiden voyage! The staff down below declare that that is nothing to what she will do when she gets into proper running trim.

It has been hard to realise that the *Majestic* has been going so fast. The passengers are all delighted with her, and lost in wonderment over her lofty public and state rooms, her luxurious elegance and stillness. My bedroom steward, a braw Scotsman, says she will soon be known as the 'Lady of the Lake'. The dining saloon is like a huge mayoral banqueting hall. The lounge is beyond words and the dome so lofty that the acoustics are as good as at any concert hall in London. Here there is afternoon tea, and at night the floor carpet is lifted, and below is a big parquet dancing floor, where we had a ball every night. On Sunday forenoon Divine service was conducted by Dr Beaumont, senior surgeon of the ship, assisted by Mr. Parton, of the London office, and a choir of the stewards. Most of the passengers were present, including Mr. Sanderson, the chairman of the White Star directors; Mr. Cauty, Liverpool manager; Lord Inchcape; Mr. Harland and Mr. Wilding, of Harland & Wolff, besides other managers and superintendents connected with the line.

My friend, Peggy Wilson, says the palm court is a 'dream' of beauty. Mr. MacDonald, a veteran Atlantic traveller, declares that the restaurant beats London and Paris for comfort and cuisine. The huge swimming pool is crowded all day and the mixed bathing is a great success. In the gallery all round it friends are gathered to see the fun. The smoke room is a marvel of elegance, and at six very big windows you can sit at ease and look out on the open sea ahead. The big 'candy store' as the Americans call it, has done a roaring business. The electric baths are popular and the gymnasium is full all day long. The children's playroom is another feature.

Though there are three sets of lifts to take you up and down from A to F decks, it is easy to lose your way, and if you wish to meet a friend you have to make a special appointment for time and place. Coming back in July, I think I will invest in a 'scooter' or roller skates to get round the big promenade deck …

Give my love to all the folks. My chum Bert says 'The *Majestic* for me every time', and that is just what I feel like, too.

Fred.

Majestic steamed into New York harbour on the afternoon of 16 May 1922. 'Sirens blew and flags dipped as the 56,000-ton liner, majestic in appearance as well as in name, passed by on the way to its pier, the longest in port. From the battery to the White Star piers at the foot of Twenty-Third Street, thousands waved from office windows and wharfs. Overhead aero marine planes encircled and acted as an aerial escort.' She had done the crossing in five days fourteen hours and forty-five minutes at an average speed of 22.7 knots, an impressive performance in itself. (Harold Sanderson told reporters: 'The ship can steam twenty-five knots easily; how much more we do not know nor do we intend to find out for the present. There will be no attempt to push the vessel.')

Her manoeuvrability won 'the greatest admiration from observers':

Under the command of Captain Sir Bertram Hayes, with Pilot A.H. Peterson, the ship accomplished a feat seldom attempted by large steamers, namely turning around in the Narrows after weighing anchor at the conclusion of the Quarantine examination. Usually vessels proceed out to Gravesend Bay where there is plenty of room to negotiate a sweeping turn around. But the *Majestic*, as if swung on a pivot, with only one tug assisting, swung around in the half-mile wide Narrows and started upstream.

One hour and fifteen minutes after weighing anchor the *Majestic* had warped into her pier and the gangplank was down. The actual docking, which means the time the beam was off the pier until the vessel was tied up, required only twenty-five minutes.

The *New York Times* said 'a favourable tide made the berthing of the ship a comparatively easy task. Ten tugs, dwarfs pitting their strength against a giant, puffed away in turning the *Majestic* into the pier slip …' Unfortunately, *Majestic*'s bow hit the corrugated side of the shed at the pier head and, even though she was hardly moving, 15ft of the shed covering was torn away. Her stern overhung the pier by about 30ft. When night drew in, red lights warned river craft to keep clear.

'Everything went well during the passage out,' Commodore Hayes recalled. The press offered their congratulations on an excellent crossing: 'It was suggested by shipping men that the *Majestic* bids fair to be a contender with the Cunarder *Mauretania* for the speed record across the Atlantic. The *Mauretania* made a trip in four days ten hours and forty-one minutes.' She was recorded as having made the fastest maiden voyage of a large liner from Cherbourg, but Hayes told reporters:

We just let the *Majestic* loaf along; there was no attempt to push her. She handles well and we experienced no trouble on the way over. We are after no speed records. Our job is to carry passengers safely across the Atlantic.

The newspapers devoted extensive coverage to the new ship, noting that the Pompeian swimming bath was 830 sq ft in size. Invitations were sent out for the ship to be inspected on the following day and many people took advantage. *Majestic* was readied for the eastbound leg of her maiden voyage, departing 20 May 1922 – no mean feat given that there were only a few days to get her prepared. The *New York Times* reported 'many notables' were sailing eastbound, including Dr J.C.A. Everwijn, a Dutch minister and his wife, and Arthur Balfour (the British steel magnate and not the former Prime Minister).

As *Majestic* moved through the Narrows on her departure, there was a sad note, as a steerage passenger jumped off the ship's stern. Despite a search, no trace was found. Thus the voyage got off to a particularly sad start, but it was otherwise a great success. Overall, 1,814 passengers were aboard (521 first class, 551 second class and 769 third class), much better than the westbound crossing. This time *Olympic* took second place to *Majestic* in the passenger stakes, for she had 1,611 passengers aboard when she made her next New York departure. *Majestic* took five days and thirteen hours to cover 3,137 miles, at an average speed of 23.6 knots. Her officers noted she had been delayed ten hours due to fog. She consumed 4,443 tons of oil fuel. During the crossing she reportedly reached the astonishing top speed of 27.1 knots for a period of some hours. All the indications are that her performance was very impressive but, even with an obliging current, it seems unlikely that she could have gone so fast. A report from London on 26 May 1922 said '*Majestic* passed Lizard Head at 9.10 o'clock this morning'. She arrived at Southampton the following morning.

Harold Sanderson was certainly pleased with the new ship, commenting:

… the *Majestic* has shown herself a very satisfactory ship in all respects, and, though there is quite a little to do in regard to small details in order to bring her up to the required standard, the work involved covers only odds and ends, and there is nothing which will prove of any great magnitude.

The *New York Times* reported that *Majestic* had failed 'by a day to beat the *Mauretania*'s record, but [a] race is denied'. The paper repeated the claim that she had reached 27.1 knots: 'During this speeding up the absence of vibration was said to have been so complete that passengers were not aware that the speed had been increased.' Her officers 'declined to discuss the trip saying they were too tired'. Sanderson's comments were more believable than the press reports.

'We have purposely never developed anything like full power', he claimed in a letter to Cunard's Sir Thomas Royden. '[*Majestic*] will, for the time being, be working under instructions not to develop engine power in excess of what is required to give her a speed of twenty-five knots, which is well below her maximum. I think the greatest power developed so far is 87,000hp, the builders' maximum being 100,000.'

Plenty of press interest in *Majestic* kept her in the news, reporting on impressive passenger lists and notable names aboard. There was a dramatic episode when she left New York on her second eastbound crossing on 17 June 1922. The *New York Times* headlined an article: 'Seized on *Majestic*; Ship Held at Hook.' The New York police received a telegram from the sheriff of Bakersfield County, California, that passenger William B. Cheeseborough was wanted 'on charges of grand larceny and abandonment'. Cheeseborough intended to sail on *Majestic*, but she was scheduled to sail at noon:

Detectives William Callahan and William Hooks jumped into an automobile at Police Headquarters and ordered the chauffeur to break all speed laws in getting to Pier 59, North River, foot of West Fourteenth Street. The detectives reached the pier a few minutes before the ocean liner was scheduled to sail. While Callahan boarded the vessel and began a search among the passengers on board, Hooks scanned the crowd on the pier.

Hooks boarded the vessel just as the gangplank was pulled away and at once began to hunt for Cheeseborough while Callahan proceeded on. Callahan completed his search for Cheeseborough among the steerage passengers, enlisting the aid of the *Majestic*'s crew. Scores of cabin boys were sent throughout the ship paging Cheeseborough.

While the search was going on the *Majestic* backed out of her dock and headed down the river.

Realising they would have to complete their search quickly or be carried across the ocean, the detectives appealed to the captain of the ocean liner. A radio message was sent to Police Headquarters and transmitted to the police boat, *John F. Hylan*, which immediately started at full speed from the Battery to overtake the liner.

The police boat sighted the *Majestic* … the *Hylan*'s whistle was kept going to attract the attention of the captain of the steamship. As the *Majestic* reached the [Scotland] Light, the detectives found Cheeseborough chatting with a group of passengers on D-deck.

… The detectives with their prisoner climbed down the side of the *Majestic* to the pilot boat by means of a Jacob's ladder. The police boat a few minutes later met the pilot boat, and Callahan and Hooks with Cheeseborough boarded the *Hylan* … Cheeseborough, although admitting his identity, denied the charges contained in the telegram by the Bakersfield County Sheriff.

An excellent cartoon of C. B. Lancaster, purser of the world's largest ship, the Majestic, by Seabrook, Southampton

Majestic's Purser Claude Lancaster, shown in a period cartoon. The commentary is highlighting the considerable value of the items he was charged with keeping secure and referring to the hyper-inflation experienced in Germany in the early 1920s. When he retired at the end of 1936 at the age of 59, the *New York Times* noted he had been a purser on White Star's first *Majestic* back in 1901. During the war, he was shipwrecked twice (*Britannic* in 1916 and *Justicia* in 1918). He had a large staff. In September 1922, he had in his department Second Purser B. Barlett; Assistant Purser W.J. Haywood; Purser's Clerk S. Cook; Purser's Clerk G. Wiseman; Purser's Clerk L. Cummins; and Purser's Clerk R. Ellis. The ship's passengers undoubtedly kept them busy. (Günter Bäbler collection)

Majestic List of Officers, 27 September 1922	
Sir Bertram F. Hayes	Master
E.L. Trant	Assistant Master
J. Binks	Chief Mate
F. Cross	First Mate
H.S. Freeman	Second Mate
L. Howarth	Third Mate
W. Poustie	Fourth Mate
J. Heenan	Fifth Mate
F. Butcher	Sixth Mate

Table: *Majestic*'s commander and his officers were all experienced, long-serving seamen. A number of her officers went on to attain their own command. Prior to taking charge of *Majestic*, Captain Sir Bertram Fox Hayes (1866–1941) had commanded *Olympic* for the longest period out of any of her commanders; Hayes' assistant commander, Edgar Lukeman Trant (1874–1958), went on to command both *Olympic* and *Majestic*; and Chief Officer John William Binks (1874–1939) also went on to attain his own command and served as *Olympic*'s master immediately prior to his retirement.

Over the summer of 1922, *Majestic* attracted more passengers and became one of the most popular ships on the Atlantic. She carried 728 passengers on her second westbound crossing and took 2,153 bookings on her eastbound return (consisting of 788 first-class passengers, 737 second-class passengers and 628 third-class passengers). *Majestic* covered the 3,055 miles of the outward passage in five days twelve hours and forty-eight minutes, at an average of 23 knots; then returned in five days nine hours and forty-two minutes, covering 3,139 miles at the mighty average of 24.2 knots. A total of 980 passengers were carried on her third outward crossing, and she arrived in New York on 4 July 1922; 1,953 passengers returned on the eastbound voyage. Her first-class list numbered 788 passengers again, a figure that surpassed *Olympic*'s best list that year of 731 first-class travellers.

'Every voyage I make on her creates a stronger impression than ever that she is a great and wonderful ship – a marvel for size, speed, steadiness and comfort,' wrote *Majestic*'s chief surgeon, Dr John C.H. Beaumont, in his memoirs. 'After her first three successful crossings, she jumped at once into popularity, and each voyage adds to her friends and admirers, the great majority of whom declare that she has spoiled them all to such an extent that they cannot think of crossing the Atlantic on any other vessel.' He thought she was 'remarkably steady' in bad weather: 'It has become a byword that, even during a day's run of 600 miles it is hard to believe that one is at sea at all. Recently, during a heavy gale from the west, with the ship heading into tremendous seas, one hundred people were dancing …' A female passenger described *Majestic* as 'so homelike'. She found 'comfort and dignity, and everything seems to run so smoothly. No noise, no shouting, no rushing around. One's wants seem attended to almost as soon as they are expressed … It is all very wonderful.'

King George V and Queen Mary finished their week at the Cowes Regatta by inspecting *Majestic* on 5 August 1922.

Harold Sanderson and Commodore Hayes welcomed them aboard. Press reports said 'the royal visitors took particular interest in the Roman swimming pool on the F-deck of the *Majestic* and in the exhibition of Winnie Elliott, the swimming Instructor. Her tricks included an imitation of a turtle having a sun bath and a submarine with [her] leg as a periscope.' Winnie explained her 'turtle trick' to an interested reporter: 'In this, I lie face downward in the water with my feet and arms out of the water, and while the body remains stationary I turn my fingers and toes in and out.' King George was impressed. Queen Mary was more interested in *Majestic*'s pantry. She asked for the labour-saving gadgets to be explained to her. Press reports emphasised that these included the can-opener and mechanical slicing machines. One of the lifeboats, filled with seamen, was lowered all the way down to the water and then rowed away. It was lowered so quickly that King George asked Commodore Hayes: 'You would not lower passengers as rapidly as that, would you?' Hayes replied that he hoped that they would never have to lower the lifeboats with passengers in them. ('Needless to say, the boat was under perfect control all the time,' Hayes wrote later.)

On the bridge, 'the King took a very great interest in everything, especially in the Clay's patent device for locking the wheel, so that the helmsman cannot turn it in any way other than that ordered, and in the "Clear View Screens", pieces of glass revolving at a high rate of speed which throw off rain or snow so that the glass remains clear under all conditions of weather'. Queen Mary was not so impressed: 'It is no better than the squeegees we have on our car.' On their way around they looked down into the engine room from the platform on E-deck, where Chief Engineer Wolff was ready to answer any questions. Queen Mary asked to see the third-class accommodation and Harold Sanderson was happy to help. She complimented him and Commodore Hayes on the general condition of the accommodation, as the tour came

THE OCEAN FERRY

With King George and Queen Mary on Board the Majestic

Majestic and the Royal Visit were featured prominently in IMM's journal *The Ocean Ferry*. (*The Ocean Ferry*, 1922/ Author's collection)

The captions read:

1. The *Majestic* off the Royal Yacht Squadron, Cowes, with the King's launch in the middle distance.
2. Sir Bertram Hayes leads the way to the bridge, the King and Queen following.
3. The King is interested in appliances on the bridge – left to right on the platform, King George, Sir Bertram Hayes, the Marquise d'Hautpoul.
4. The King looks down to the water from the bridge – the distance is 80 feet.
5. The royal party above the engine room. The Queen is looking down at the giant turbines, and the King upward through the third stack, which is as tall as a ten-story [*sic*] building. At the left is Joseph Wolff, chief engineer of the ship.
6. Miss Winnie Elliott, the *Majestic*'s 'official mermaid,' who swam for the King and Queen in the great tank of the ship's Pompeian bath.
8. [*sic*] Inspection of the ship's company. The Queen is shown speaking to Miss Elliott, the first figure at the left. The last two figures on the right are A.B. Cauty, Joint Manager of the White Star Line, Liverpool, and Sir Bertram Hayes.

to an end after one-and-a-half hours. 'The King and Queen lunched in the Parisian restaurant on the B-deck and had their photographs taken,' according to the *New York Times*. Photos of the Royal visitors were presented to the ship and adorned the main companionway. They remained a considerable source of interest to passengers afterwards. Harold Sanderson was 'full of satisfaction' following the visit and very pleased that it had gone 'without a hitch'.

Not everything was perfect. During a final inspection before her fifth westbound departure from Southampton on 16 August 1922, the ship's engineering staff were preparing to raise steam and uncovered defective studs in the port low pressure ahead turbine. The studs connected the 'dummy rotor to the main rotor' and were fractured. In order to repair them, they needed to drill them out and renew about thirty studs, but time was pressing and the White Star Line decided to complete repairs at sea. She had plenty of power to operate and manoeuvre safely, so the Board of Trade surveyor allowed her to sail. As a consequence, *Majestic* went to sea with only three of her propellers working ahead. The remaining propeller was fixed in position rather than revolving freely in the water, reducing her speed to 15 to 16 knots. It was only when repairs were completed several days later that her speed increased up to 24 knots and so her 1,646 passengers were somewhat delayed. By the time she returned to Southampton, the Board of Trade were concerned that the original studs had 'given trouble after such a brief period of use'. *Majestic* had only been sailing for three months. They arranged for all the studs to be replaced with fitted bolts. Oddly enough, it was hard to understand what the problem was. While she was in New York, *Majestic*'s chief engineer had been informed by a representative of the Parsons Turbine Company 'that exactly the same trouble had been experienced on the *Leviathan*; he had no satisfactory theory as to the cause'. (By 27 February 1923, the studs had all been replaced and the surveyor thought 'no further trouble is anticipated'.)

In September 1922, *Majestic* reportedly set a record for passenger numbers. She carried 838 first-class passengers and 712 people in second class – for a grand total of 1,550 'cabin' passengers. A total of 640 third-class travellers were also on board, not to mention more than 5,000 sacks of mail and $1 million in gold, destined for banks in New York. In order to examine the cabin passengers' baggage, 175 Customs Inspectors were needed. She had been in service barely half a year, but White Star were wrestling with the necessary arrangements to get her dry-docked. There was no available dry dock in the United Kingdom available to accommodate her and the floating dry dock intended for Southampton would not be in place until the summer of 1924. The only dry dock large enough was the naval dock at Boston, Massachusetts, and Harold Sanderson had written in March 1922 that, even there, 'much dredging will be required to permit of her entering the dock …' She went there in November 1922. The White Star Line took the opportunity to replace her existing propellers, which had been made out of steel due to materials shortages in Germany, with cast bronze replacements; her hull was thoroughly cleaned of marine growth and repainted; and the Board of Trade inspected her and issued a passenger certificate from 21 November 1922. (It was expensive simply to use the dry dock, with White Star incurring expenses of £21,122 when she was dry-docked in 1923.)

MAJESTIC: DRY-DOCKED AT BOSTON

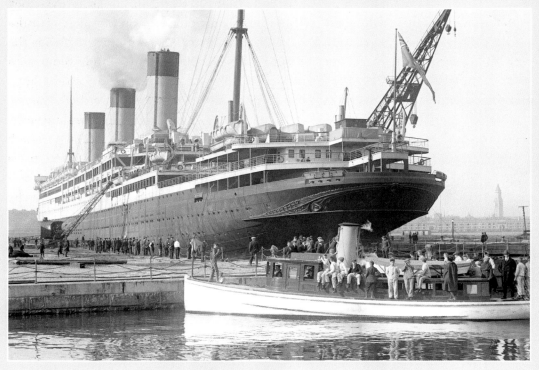

Leslie Jones (1886-1967) was a press photographer who worked for the *Boston Herald-Traveller* for decades. He had a keen eye for detail and the human interest, taking thousands of magnificent photographs and saving nearly 40,000 negatives. They included many events in and around Boston. *Majestic* was dry-docked three times at Boston, firstly in November 1922 and finally in April 1924. The images Jones captured included a wonderful view of the ship's port bow (top right); her after port side (top left) and looking forward along the port side from the ship's stern (bottom). The detail is quite amazing. The spectators aboard *Pilgrim* are visible, as is a sign at the ship's stern explaining 'Quadruple Screws Keep Clear of Blades'. There are three crewmen visible atop the third funnel. They must have had a magnificent view.

When she had been dry-docked at Boston in 1923, quite a bit of maintenance work needed doing: 'Many thousands of rivets in the flat of bottom were caulked.' Unfortunately, White Star had not taken the opportunity to arrange for a Board of Trade inspection. They ended up applying to have the passenger certificate extended considerably beyond the usual twelve months. Initially, they had sought an extension to February 1924, which was approved, but then anticipated 'it may be necessary to ask the Board to sanction further extensions, possibly up to August next [1924]'.

The passenger certificate allowed her to carry '4,124 persons' including 3,070 passengers and 1,054 crew and the Board's view was that 'if a serious casualty should happen to the vessel involving heavy loss of life it would be difficult to defend the position of permitting a vessel of this size to run without survey for a period of nine months longer than allowed by the provisions of the Merchant Shipping Acts; especially as it is mainly a matter of expense only that is at issue'. On 25 October 1923, the Board's Principal Ship Surveyor had thought 'the utmost that should be conceded in all the circumstances is another three months beyond the three months' extension ... already agreed'. That was conditional on *Majestic* being dry-docked by 21 February 1924, or a 'competent diver' examining the propellers and rudder posts and a surveyor being satisfied the hull was in good condition 'as far as can be ascertained'. (He noted later: 'it is not an uncommon experience in these large vessels, which may be driven at speed through heavy seas, to find defects revealed by drydocking which otherwise would not be brought to light, and if not made good, might seriously affect the seaworthiness of the vessel. Two cases in point are *Aquitania* and *Empress of Britain* ...')

The dry-docking in April 1924 allowed for a thorough inspection before she resumed her schedule. (Courtesy of the Boston Public Library, Leslie Jones Collection)

By the end of the 1922 she had raised her highest average speed to 24.6 knots. She returned to Southampton on 1 December 1922 after an eastbound crossing of 3,104 miles in five days six hours and thirteen minutes. The *New York Times* reported she had set a record, claiming: 'This is the fastest voyage ever made between the two ports [New York's Ambrose Channel Lightship to Cherbourg's breakwater] and it is one hour and fifty-six minutes faster than the record run of the Cunarder *Mauretania* ...' Commodore Hayes noted 'that the voyage had been made without driving the ship in any way and in ordinary November weather'. He credited the 'increased speed to the four new propellers and the scraping and painting of her hull in the naval graving dock in Boston two weeks ago'. *Majestic* 'debarked her passengers at 9 a.m.' and so they were able 'to arrive in London by special train at noon'.

She had proven herself a popular ship as well: *Majestic* carried over 26,000 passengers in 1922; her highest westbound list was 2,191 passengers and highest eastbound 2,123 passengers. Her first ten round-trip voyages set the scene for the remainder of her career. In comparison her running mate *Olympic* carried under 28,000 passengers, but she had been in service for the entire year. *Homeric* carried 24 per cent of the White Star Line's Southampton to New York passengers that year, while *Majestic*'s share was 37 per cent and *Olympic*'s 39 per cent. Her popularity led to financial success. From May to December 1922, she earned receipts of £1,142,648 (an average of £114,364.80 on each round trip) and a net profit of £332,522 (£33,252.2 on each round trip). It was a good performance and highlighted her earnings potential.

Majestic returned to Southampton early in January 1923. The *Liverpool Echo* claimed she had set 'a record number' of first-class passengers 'for the month of January' as well as bringing in 4,000 sacks of mail. (The first-class passenger list was 697 according to the North Atlantic Passenger Conference, the sort of number normally seen in high season.) Their reporter noted that Madame Marguerite Namara, the 'American prima donna', had disembarked at Cherbourg: she 'sang at a ship's concert when the collection reached nearly £200 for seamen's charities'. *Majestic* made her first westbound departure of the year on 28 February 1923. It was a slow crossing and she did not arrive in New York until 7 March, recording an average speed of only 19.61 knots. She had some very healthy first-class passenger lists both westbound and eastbound as the year wore on, including bringing 678 first-class passengers into New York on 27 March 1923.

On Sunday, 22 July 1923, the White Star Line invited 200 members of the British Medical Association to visit *Majestic*. They toured the ship's first-class accommodation and expressed 'wonderment and delight' at 'the spaciousness and elegance of the various public rooms …' Dr Beaumont gave them a tour of the medical department 'which is conveniently "en suite" at a point 240 feet from the bow, where there is no vibration':

> The consulting room, private dispensary, waiting room and operating room were a surprise to the visitors, and, still more so, all the latest appliances for surgical, medical, dental and bacteriological work. The spacious hospitals were then inspected. Of these there are eight, containing 62 beds, 42 of them being reserved for general cases and 20 for fevers, where the isolation is complete and fulfils every requirement of the British Board of Trade. In addition to these, a small ward for maternity cases and one for mental cases, both of which have frequently to be dealt with on board.
>
> In addition to the surgeon's suite forward, there is a large surgery amidships, where Dr Jones, assistant surgeon of the ship, looks after the second and third class passengers who, by this arrangement, do not come into contact with the crew and first class passengers.

Beaumont said he had performed twenty-seven anaesthetic operations during the previous year. ('In no single case had the ship ever been slowed down for a minute, although in all of them she was going at any speed from 23 to 25 knots per hour,' reported the *Hampshire Advertiser*.) 'As a matter of fact,' Beaumont explained, 'the ship is so extraordinarily steady that the question of slowing down never even occurs to me, and we proceed just as if in hospital on shore.' One of the doctors had heard that babies were often born in third class. 'Oh, yes, indeed,' Beaumont replied: 'Why not? It is a good business proposition for them. They get my services free, the company sends them at their expense to a hospital on arrival, and very often a handsome sum of money is collected for the mother by some benevolent lady in the first class.' (Some of *Majestic*'s third-class passengers had their plans disrupted on the very next voyage, because she had to land 937 of them at Boston due to congestion at Ellis Island in New York.)

The press reported fresh 'records' throughout the year. On 14 May 1923, the *Portsmouth Evening News* said *Majestic* had covered 603 miles 'at an average speed of nearly 25¾ knots an hour from noon Sunday to noon Monday. This is the *Majestic*'s best daily run on an eastbound voyage.' Eastbound crossings were usually faster because she had the current in her favour, rather than against her. A report in the *Hampshire Advertiser* five days later even claimed that *Majestic* had 'set up a new speed record between the Caskets and Cherbourg by covering the distance at an average speed of 29.7 knots':

> It is interesting to note when referring to the *Majestic*'s 29.7 knots that the White Star liner *Olympic* also made a remarkable burst of speed whilst coming up the Channel last year. On this occasion that vessel touched a speed of 27.8 knots. The 29.7 knots steamed by the *Majestic* is a remarkable achievement, and there is no figure in the whole history of the mercantile marine that can approach it.

Neither ship was remotely capable of the speeds attributed to them. Hayes explained: 'She actually covered the ground at that speed, but I would not say that she cut through the water at that speed.' If the figure was even close to being correct, she must indeed have been 'helped considerably by a strong following tide, and it is to this fact that the unprecedented speed is mainly attributable', as the reporter concluded. Even then, the tide would need to have been several knots!

What *Majestic* certainly did do was make her fastest eastbound crossing to date. She left New York on 11 August 1923 and completed the 3,202-mile crossing in five days eight hours thirty-nine minutes at an average speed of 24.89 knots. Early in November 1923, *The Scotsman* reported when *Majestic* was scheduled to arrive back at Southampton. If she was on schedule, she:

> will have created a record by making the voyage from Southampton to New York and back in a fortnight. The *Majestic* was only 25 hours at New York and in that time took 7,016 tons of oil, 4,300 tons of water and 4,030 sacks of mails on board, embarking 428 first class, in addition to the second and third class passengers, a remarkable quick turn around.

Cunard disputed the claim. The *Daily Mail* reported that *Mauretania* had 'crossed from Liverpool to New York and back in 12 days 12 hours, including a stay of 37 hours 20 minutes at New York for coaling' in 1910; and *Lusitania* 'also made the double crossing of the Atlantic … in less than 12 days'. (Strictly speaking, they were not comparing precisely like with like, because neither pre-war crossing had been from Southampton.)

Remarkably, *Majestic*'s average speed for the crossings she made in 1923 was listed as 23.29 knots by the North Atlantic Passenger Conference – identical to *Mauretania*'s. Her older sister *Leviathan* was listed as averaging 23 knots. *Mauretania*'s performances were coming under increasing scrutiny. In the early 1920s her speed performance was not that of her prewar self. Humfrey Jordan recalled:

> The *Leviathan* as well as the *Majestic* was at that time occasionally, when the weather promised well, being driven all out and making fast passages. Competition was keen and the chance to take from an old ship the record she had held for so long, looked better than it ever had before …[3]

It was not to be. The simple reality was that *Mauretania* was smaller, lighter and with a hull designed with speed in mind. Even though her propelling machinery was not as powerful as *Majestic*'s, it did not need to be. *Majestic*'s weight was much greater and she simply did not have the enormous additional power necessary to beat the Cunarder. Jordan explained: '*Leviathan* and *Majestic* and the others had to drop out of the competition; it seemed useless to go on with it.'[4] (*Mauretania* showed a turn of speed the following year: she averaged 25.6 knots westbound in August 1924 and then 26.25 knots eastbound.)

Majestic was also the most popular ship on the North Atlantic express route to New York. She carried around 16,000 passengers in first class alone, which was much more than her running mate *Homeric* carried in all three classes in 1923. The average number of first-class passengers carried by the *Majestic* was the highest on the Atlantic by far, with the *Aquitania*, *Leviathan*, *Berengaria* and *Olympic* joining her as the five most popular first-class ships. She carried 36,779 passengers in total, which was far ahead of her rivals (*Berengaria* came closest at 29,957 passengers). Her popularity certainly came to the attention of the press. On 27 October 1923, the *Liverpool Echo* had reported that: '*Majestic*, which left Southampton yesterday, is taking 2,730 passengers to New

York, the largest number the steamer has ever carried westbound.' The figures reported by the North Atlantic Passenger Conference were slightly lower: 475 first, 731 second and 1,416 third class, for a total of 2,622, but in any case it was her highest westbound passenger list to date. (Her highest westbound first-class passenger list then stood at 838 in September 1922; and her highest eastbound was 853 first-class passengers in June 1923.)[5]

She sailed from Southampton on 2 January 1924 for her first crossing of the year to New York. On board were over 1,000 passengers, including 450 first-, 338 second- and 214 third-class passengers. It was not uneventful. White Star issued a statement that she 'touched the ground off Cowes, but refloated, and proceeded on her voyage undamaged'. The Southampton correspondent of the Press Association was quoted as saying that she had grounded on soft mud at Castle Point, refloating two hours later. Then she experienced 'gales and heavy seas' and a wireless message to White Star's New York offices indicated her speed had been reduced to 8 knots 'for a whole day'. When she did arrive in New York a day late on 10 January 1924, Hayes expressed concerns about the narrowness of the channel into New York Harbour. *Leviathan* had grounded the previous month and her commander, Captain Hartley, described the 'tortuous channel and erratic tides'. Hayes said it was 'terrible to have to wind one's way up the bay against the winds, tides, and currents, and to dodge continually the small craft which dart across the steamer's path without any restriction'.

On *Majestic's* eastbound return crossing, her complement included 620 first-class passengers. Once she had completed her second round trip for the year, she was joined by *Olympic*, which returned to service in mid-February 1924 after an extensive winter overhaul. (*Homeric* did not resume sailing until 30 April 1924. *White Star Magazine* noted that she had been converted to oil burning by Harland & Wolff,

at a cost of £250,000. One of the benefits was a moderate increase in her speed.) Late in February 1924, press reports appeared of a 'mysterious fire on *Majestic*' in the stewards' quarters: 'Workmen noticed smoke pouring from the ventilation holes of a wardrobe and immediately they broke the door open [and] a tongue of flame shout [recte: shot] out'. The fire authorities at Southampton docks were alerted and extinguished the fire but there were 'suspicious circumstances which the police are investigating'.

The shipping lines faced many challenges. On 16 April 1924, Cunard held their annual general meeting in Liverpool. Sir Thomas Royden explained that 'the average cost of oil fuel in 1923 shows an increase over the average cost in 1922'. He noted 'that the cost of fuel forms nearly thirty per cent of our total voyage expenses'. The shipping lines faced a challenge to keep their costs down. Early in May 1924, the *Journal of Commerce* said that White Star's annual report for 1923 showed it had 'passed through a period of exceptional difficulty, with working results much less favourable than those of previous years'. The United States government had enacted immigration restrictions in 1921 and further restrictions followed in 1924. These had 'a very unfavourable effect on passenger business generally, particularly with regard to third class travel'. Higher wages added to higher fuel costs. White Star faced challenges on the Australian service, too. They reduced their dividend from £625,000 in 1922 to £250,000 in 1923: 'It has obviously been a difficult year, but the management has proved capable of overcoming adverse trading conditions before …' (Cunard had reduced their dividend to £222,810 for 1923.)

Focusing on third-class passenger numbers westbound on the Southampton to New York express service, *Adriatic* and *Olympic* had carried 17,941 third-class passengers in 1920. *Olympic*, *Homeric* and *Majestic* together carried 8,447 in 1922; 13,766 in 1923; and a mere 5,962 in 1924. The total number had fallen steeply. Moreover, the average third-class passenger list westbound fell from 997 in 1920 to 153 in 1924. (The eastbound numbers fared somewhat better.) In terms of overall passenger numbers, *Majestic* went on to carry over 34,000 in 1924 and marked another year ahead of her rivals. An article in *White Star* magazine noted: 'The world's largest liner embarked 2,127 passengers at New York on June 28th, the biggest Eastbound total [so far] this year; 884 of these were in the first class, this figure being the highest for Eastbound travellers ever conveyed, first class, across the Atlantic.' Early in July 1924, Southampton's Palace Theatre held 'the Grand Majestic Night':

> The Palace was not only packed with an enthusiastic audience, but it was specially decorated in honour of the gala attended by the Commander, Officers, and crew of the world's largest liner. Among those present were the Major and Mayoress of Southampton, Commodore Sir Bertram Hayes, K.C.M.G., D.S.O., and Mr P.E. Curry (Southampton Manager of the White Star Line).

Performers from *Majestic* supplemented the programme and Commodore Hayes was presented with a 'handsome bouquet by the most minute bell boy of the *Majestic*'. Two days later, *Majestic* departed Southampton. Rev. J. Hemery was a passenger and his friends sang hymns from the dockside. Not all publicity was good publicity. On 23 July 1924, *The Scotsman* reported on a court case brought before the King's Bench Division in London. Ernest Cadbury Jones had claimed damages 'for personal injuries received' as an eastbound passenger aboard *Majestic* in September 1923. His left hand had been 'badly crushed in the porthole glass of his cabin'. A special jury awarded him £1,073, but then 'argument arose on legal points regarding the question of the defendant's [White Star's] liability under the terms of

the contract, and how far American law applied'. One of the conditions attached to the passenger ticket was that White Star 'should not be held liable for the neglectful acts of their servants'. The Lord Chief Justice 'did not think they could evade responsibility on that ground', but unfortunately Jones had not lodged his 'notice of claim' in the required time. The judge upheld White Star's position and ruled in their favour but hoped 'they would take into consideration the question of compensating the plaintiff'.

Although the shipping lines faced economic challenges, two years after she finally entered service *Majestic* was undoubtedly a great asset for White Star. Unfortunately, in the summer of 1924 the first signs began to appear that pointed to serious problems ahead. On 14 June 1924, water was discovered in a first-class stateroom on the port side. The cause was a crack in the deck plating, which was 10½in long and hard to see from the underside. On 2 August 1924, another crack was discovered 'at the middle of the deck' and finally extended to the openings in the deck for the passenger lifts. The Board of Trade's Senior Ship Surveyor thought that the first crack was itself 'serious and should have been explored' at the time. However, *Majestic* continued in service. A report of casualty noted damage incurred 'between 28 October and 4 November 1924'. She 'ran into heavy weather and dangerous seas. [One] port [hole] broken and another strained.'

On Tuesday, 9 December 1924, *Majestic* left Southampton for New York with 1,246 passengers. The *Southampton Times* reported that she was 'due at New York on Monday [15 December]' and:

> will make a very quick turn round, as she will leave for England on Wednesday, serving as the Christmas ship. She is due at Southampton on the Tuesday before Christmas day. Thus the round voyage of 6,000 miles will be completed in exactly a fortnight, including a 48 hour stay in New

York … It is anticipated that the steamer will bring a very large number of English people home to spend Christmas in the old country. The *Majestic* is taking 8,500 bags of mail to New York and it is likely that she will have a record mail of Christmas wishes when she next reaches Southampton.

By the night of Sunday, 14 December 1924, she was a day away from New York. She was running at high speed through heavy seas when a report 'like a cannon shot' rang out: a third much more serious fracture had occurred. The C-deck plating had fractured from the inside of the starboard second funnel uptake right across the deck, through the port side second funnel uptake and out to the ship's side, continuing to the heavy plating at the side of the ship (the sheer strake) and down the ship's side (see page 76). Fortunately, she reached New York safely the following afternoon. Her average speed for the crossing was 22.1 knots. On arrival, the fracture 'was open ¼ inch at [the] top of sheer strake, and off to nothing at the lowest rivet, leaving an unbroken piece below the rivet'. When she took on thousands of tons of oil fuel for the return crossing and settled lower in the water, the fracture closed up.[6]

Majestic left New York on 17 December 1924 carrying 1,164 passengers. Unsurprisingly, the fracture opened up again as the voyage continued 'and finally extended to the bottom edge of the inner sheer strake'. She completed the crossing at an average speed of 23.5 knots. Officials from the White Star Line and Harland & Wolff came on board at Cherbourg 'for the purpose of surveying the damage' and, when she docked at Southampton on the evening of 23 December 1924, Senior Ship Surveyor O'Sullivan joined them from the Board of Trade's office on Canute Road. He found serious damage: 'C-deck was seen to be fractured at dead amidships from the inner side of the starboard funnel uptake to the extreme port side of the deck and, further, the sheer strake was fractured.' Leaky rivets were also found in

the deck plating on the starboard side of the funnel uptake: 'The damage is very serious, and it was evident that the vessel had been experiencing very heavy weather and seas.' The sheer strake plating at the side of the ship and the deck plating on C-deck, which was the strength deck, were significant because they formed the uppermost part of the hull. The sudden, extensive fracturing represented a serious structural failure. White Star were told *Majestic* 'could not be allowed to proceed to sea until repairs were carried out' and the Board of Trade revoked *Majestic*'s passenger certificate.

On 24 December 1924, the *Southern Daily Echo* reported:

Owing to unforeseen circumstance the White Star Line have decided to take the *Majestic* off the service for overhaul earlier than was originally intended and consequently the sailing of the vessel from Southampton on December 31st has been cancelled. Arrangements are being made for the *Lapland* to fill the gap.

Three days later, the newspaper clarified: 'Her next sailing has been cancelled owing to the fact that on her last homeward trip a slight vertical crack developed in her plates high above the waterline. In the circumstances it was decided to repair the vessel immediately. The work is expected to take about two months to complete.' They said 'the damage is not in the least alarming. It is not an unusual occurrence for steamers when experiencing rough weather to develop cracks in their hulls …' Certainly, it was completely true that ships were damaged by heavy weather, but the report belied the extent and seriousness of the damage. (It was Hayes' final voyage before retiring. He was presented with a number of gifts from his crew, including one from Chief Engineer Wolff, a 'magnificently fitted wardrobe and a silver fitted dressing case' from the Catering Department, and another present from the chief stewardess.)

The naval architectural firm Roscoe & Little, based in the Royal Liver Building in Liverpool, prepared several options for schemes of repair, including the minimum necessary repairs; the repairs needed to restore *Majestic* to her previous strength; and the repairs needed to make her significantly stronger and 'practically eliminate the possibility of a recurrence of the trouble'. The first scheme was 'the most economical and the least that can be done in the circumstances' and 'would make the vessel's strength substantially the same as when acquired by the White Star Line', but leave her 'some twenty per cent weaker than *Olympic*, assuming of course that the original steel [on *Majestic*] was equal to [the standard of] British Lloyds [Classification Society]'. They warned similar trouble might happen again in future. Instead, White Star and Harland & Wolff opted for substantial repairs to make *Majestic* stronger than she had been originally.

It became clear there were multiple factors that had caused the problem. Roscoe & Little understood that the original builders' specification was for a designed draft of 35ft 6in or a displacement of 57,700 tons, but *Majestic* had been running at a draft of 38ft 6in to 39ft or a displacement of 61,200 to 62,200 tons: 'This means an excess of 7 to 8 per cent in the stresses above the designed stress.' To make matters worse 'we understand that, even at 35ft 6in draft, the original owners [HAPAG] did not intend the vessel to be used in the winter North Atlantic service'. When the test results on samples of *Majestic*'s steel plating came back to the Board of Trade, they showed a 'surprising deficiency of tensile strength': plating from the sheer strake bore only 23.2 to 25.4 tons, whereas the new replacement plating went to 32.5 to 34.5 tons, which was in line with requirements.

The Principal Ship Surveyor pointed out that splitting the funnel uptakes into two 'and carrying them up on opposite sides of the vessel involves cutting into the stiffer parts of the strength deck plating'. It was a great design feature as far as the passenger accommodation was concerned, but the designers had not incorporated sufficient additional strengthening in order to compensate. When *Majestic* had entered service, the Board of Trade's calculations of her strength 'were consistent with the results of the calculations made in the case of the *Olympic* which has, I think, proved to be a successful ship in the matter of strength'. Nonetheless, initial calculations early in January 1925 showed that, owing to *Majestic*'s greater weight and length, her tendency to bend ('bending moment' in naval architectural terms) was 33 per cent greater than *Olympic*'s. The problem was that her strength was only increased by 27 per cent, or a mere 13.5 per cent once the calculations accounted for the split funnel uptakes and lift openings. She was comparatively weaker. Senior Ship Surveyor Sullivan reported:

> The poor plating, the bad arrangement of deck openings, and the driving of the vessel in heavy weather were primarily responsible for the damage. The poor plating upsets any calculations based on the strength of plating ordinarily used in ships. The deck openings could have been designed differently by putting the lifts in another position and avoiding the ventilator openings at the corner of the funnel uptakes … The driving of the vessel is a matter which, I understand, has been seriously discussed by the owners' representatives …

White Star issued an instruction specific to *Majestic*: 'In view of the exceptional conditions attending the navigation of this steamer during heavy weather, the commander is desired to satisfy himself that the officers fully understand those conditions, and he is also desired to issue to them the necessary instructions to prevent any undue strain being placed on the steamer or engines under such circumstances.'

Repair work started quickly. Harland & Wolff strengthened C-deck from 112ft forward to 121ft aft of the fracture, strengthening the ship over a total of 233ft. The plating on the inner side of the lifts was originally doubled but the replacement plating was trebled in thickness and included substantially thicker steel plates; similarly, the middle line was changed from single to doubled plating. Then, with the deck repaired, they began to repair the port sheer strake at the side of the ship and only started repairing the starboard side later, taking 'every care'. Altogether, some 280 tons of new plating was worked into the ship and the net increase in weight worked out to 160 tons. On Sunday, 22 March 1925, they conducted an inclining experiment and the results were 'practically as before', because extra pumps were fitted lower down in the hull which 'counterbalanced the increased hull weight'. Five days later, the Board of Trade did the first of several surveys. They were worried there might be damage at the bottom of the hull attributable to the failure above but did not find anything, although hundreds of rivets needed caulking. The Board of Trade Surveyor reported: 'The whole of the work has been very carefully and thoroughly carried out and I have never seen better work. It reflects the greatest credit on Messrs. Harland & Wolff and their workmen. Every precaution in my opinion has been taken to render the *Majestic* safe and seaworthy.'

The Board kept *Majestic* on their 'confidential list' for ongoing monitoring. (White Star certainly spent plenty of money. For the first six months of 1925, they charged *Majestic*'s operating account no less than £36,275 for 'layup expenses at Southampton'; £4,291 for 'overhaul charges' and £26,812 for 'repairs' undertaken by Harland & Wolff.) On 9 April 1925, the *Southern Daily Echo* reported *Majestic* was safely out of the floating dry dock: 'The operation of sinking the mammoth dock commenced at 7.30 this morning with the flooding of the bottom pontoon and the side walls. Steadily, 82,000 tons of water poured into the compartments and slowly the dock sank. The vessel was afloat at ten o'clock … the tugs took charge and towed her out … An hour later the *Majestic* was at her berth in the docks.' She was ready to resume her place as the most popular ship afloat.

5

THE PEAK YEARS

'As the giant liner moved slowly from the quayside this morning she presented a perfect picture,' wrote the *Southern Daily Echo*. 'The *Majestic*'s glistening white superstructure contrasting splendidly with the jet black of her hull made her a stately "Queen of the Sea".' *Majestic* had a new commander, Captain R.G. Metcalfe, who was 'proud' of *Majestic*. He had been at sea for thirty-eight years, twenty-eight of them with the White Star Line, commanding ships including *Cretic*, *Romanic*, *Ceramic*, *Baltic*, *Cedric*, *Adriatic* and *Homeric*. She brought 736 passengers (390 in first class, 179 second, and 167 third) over to New York. Her time was respectable and she completed the crossing in five days eighteen hours and thirty minutes, at an average speed of 23.1 knots. By the time she arrived in New York eager observers had gathered to give a 'rousing welcome' as she steamed up the bay. 'Small craft in the harbour saluted her all the way from Quarantine to her dock at the foot of West Seventeenth Street.' International Mercantile Marine Company (IMM) president Philip Franklin was among the passengers and was eager to speak to reporters:

> The *Majestic* has been entirely reconditioned, and is in perfect condition throughout. In fact, she is better today than when she was new. Her time on the present voyage, which was a rough one, was entirely satisfactory.

During the voyage, White Star's Southampton Superintendent Engineer Blake and Harland & Wolff's F.C. Dunlop were aboard to monitor her performance. There are no records of any concerns. Sadly the voyage was marred by the death of Anna Haluska, a 73-year-old passenger on her way to America with her grandson and granddaughter, two days out of Southampton. Senior Surgeon Dr John C.H. Beaumont diagnosed a cerebral haemorrhage, and she was buried at sea the following night, 24 April 1925. *Majestic* was soon ready to sail eastbound and she left New York on 2 May 1925. Her passengers included William Wrigley, the chewing gum manufacturer. He said trade was not affected by economic circumstances: 'People chew harder when they are sad.' Her sister *Leviathan* sailed several hours later. Speculation that they would 'race' was dismissed by the *New York Times* but *Majestic* made her fastest ever eastbound crossing, completing 3,241 miles in five days nine hours and forty minutes at an average of 25 knots. (*Leviathan* averaged 24.63 knots.) It was all the more impressive because she had left port with a draft of 39ft 4in, so she was by no means lightly loaded. Metcalfe was 'full of praise for his new ship': 'he had no hesitation in stating that the *Majestic* was the most wonderful ship afloat'. The 'splendid crew' impressed him and worked well across the departments.[1]

On 2 September 1925, *Majestic* backed out of the Ocean Dock and departed Southampton successfully. Family and friends waved her off. She arrived in New York on 8 September 1925, bringing in 2,398 passengers (including 860 in first class). Four days later, she left New York for the eastbound crossing with 810 passengers. Westbound passenger traffic was always higher in September, whereas it was a quieter time of year for eastbound traffic. (PA Images/Alamy Stock Photo)

THE BRIDGE OF S.S.MAJESTIC - GREATEST SHIP IN WORLD 9/9/25 / MINE IN HANSON. N.Y.City.

Four snapshots of *Majestic* at New York, taken on 9 September 1925. Top left, clockwise: *Majestic*'s bridge; looking aft along the ship's starboard hull, the doubled plating and strong hydraulic riveting is visible; looking aft over the ship's stern; and part of the first-class promenade deck space. (Mike Poirier collection)

Although she had missed the earlier part of the year due to her lay-up for repairs, *Majestic* did very well in 1925. While she completed only twelve round trips to New York, she carried 28,630 passengers at an average of nearly 1,200 per crossing; she had a higher average number of passengers eastbound than her sisters, and she had the second-best westbound.[2] The year was not without its share of troubles. When she departed from Southampton with 2,398 passengers on 2 September 1925, she was nearly delayed by a seamen's strike, until White Star signed on replacements for those crewmen who had refused to sail.[3] Her popularity continued as the 1920s wore on: between her maiden voyage in 1922 and the end of 1927 she carried just under 202,000 passengers at an average of just over 1,250 per crossing.[4] She carried more passengers in total than any other ship in 1923, 1924, 1926 and 1928, only losing in 1925 because she was not in service the entire year. (*Leviathan* did extraordinarily well in 1927.) In 1926, total revenue reached an all-time peak and she made £702,080 in gross operating profit. Profits stabilised at a slightly lower level each year until 1930.

White Star tried to attract passengers of modest means and alleviate the reduction in third-class traffic by selling 'tourist third cabin' tickets (between second and third class). On 30 June 1925, *Majestic* arrived in New York with her first passengers – all forty-three of them. On her return, she carried 542 tourist third cabin passengers, but then she only carried them westbound until September 1925; she did not carry any more the following year until her eastbound departure from New York on 5 June 1926. In 1926, White Star's three express ships carried 8,493 third-class and 3,769 tourist third cabin passengers in total, a combined average of 279 per crossing. They were grappling with plans to replace the smaller, slower *Homeric* with a new ship. On 4 August 1926, the *New York Times* quoted IMM president Philip Franklin as saying, 'We are proceeding with the preparation of plans and specifications for a new mammoth steamer of the *Majestic–Olympic* class.' He said she would be 'about 60,000 gross tons', with the same speed as *Majestic* and would 'probably be called the

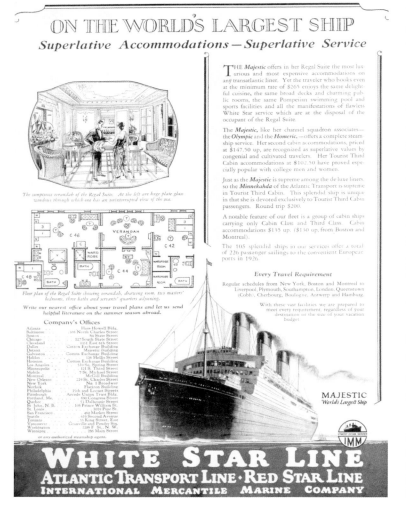

A stylish advertisement from February 1926. IMM advertised various services through the Atlantic Transport, Red Star and White Star Lines under its own banner ('utmost ocean service'). White Star's flagship was the highlight, with 'superlative accommodation' on board the world's largest liner. (Author's collection)

Oceanic'. He estimated she would take three and a half years to build.

Another issue was that IMM was looking to sell its controlling interest in the White Star Line. In July 1925 Sir Frederick Lewis (later Lord Essendon) of Furness Withy & Co. suggested to Cunard's Sir Thomas Royden that their companies should jointly make an effort to acquire IMM's British vessels. Sir Thomas initially agreed. Then IMM informed Sir Frederick that there were others interested and Sir Thomas 'said that his interests would not agree to being played off against any third party'. By March 1926, Sir Thomas had been asked whether the Cunard Line would be disposed to buying its long-time rival, White Star. He concluded that Cunard should not increase its stake in the North Atlantic passenger business. Meanwhile, Furness Withy & Co. had sought to buy White Star on the condition that the Oceanic Steam Navigation Co. Ltd shares showed a return of at least 8 per cent. The return was not that good and so the sale did not go through. In November 1926 Lord Kylsant's Royal Mail Steam Packet Co. purchased the White Star Line for £7 million (excluding interest payments). The first £2 million was due before 1 February 1927, with instalments in June 1928 and June 1929, and the final payment of £2.5 million due before 21 December 1936. There was plenty to celebrate with White Star back under full British control but, beneath the surface, Kylsant's shipping empire was experiencing increasing financial strains that would, ultimately, lead to its break-up.

The express service continued much as normal. There were some sad events on board. On 9 July 1926, *Majestic* was a day out of Cherbourg when Assistant Butcher John Clydesdale 'committed suicide by jumping overboard and was drowned'. Several passengers saw him strike the ship's rail and fall into the sea. The engines were stopped and the ship circled round but there was no sign of him. On 25 August 1926, Steward Thomas Archer Ives cut his throat with a razor blade in the stewards' quarters and passed away despite the best efforts of the ship's medical staff. Two months later, in the early hours of 13 October 1926, first-class passenger David P. Davis fell overboard. Lucile Gehring was with him the previous evening from dinner onwards. Davis occupied first-class staterooms D42 and D44 and they went to D42, the suite's sitting room. They sat talking and 'had an occasional drink' (a quart bottle of champagne between them) and Davis drank 'half a bottle of rye whiskey'. Davis' 10-year-old son, George, was asleep in the room next door. Lucile 'tried to leave on three separate occasions but he pulled her back after she had reached the door'. (Night watchman R.W. Tyrell 'did not intervene as

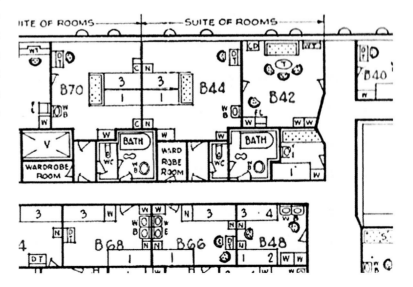

One of *Majestic*'s first-class 'suite of rooms' on the port side of D-deck, comprising a bedroom (D44) and sitting room (D42), wardrobe room and private bathroom facilities. The location of the sofa and the two portholes is clearly visible in the sitting room. David P. Davis' son, George, was asleep in the bedroom when his father plunged to his death. (The deck designation later changed from D-deck to B-deck, as shown on this 1933 deckplan, so that B42 became D42 and B44 became D44). (Author's collection)

there was no violence and he knew the parties to be friends, who sat late as a rule'.) Davis remarked: 'If you go away and leave me, I'll go through there,' and pointed through the porthole. She thought it was 'bravado'. He put his money on the table and 'told her to keep it as she'd need it'. He 'sat for a time in the recess of the port with his feet on the sofa'. She was 'somewhat confused' what happened next. He said 'catch me honey, I'm slipping' and 'goodbye dearie here I go'. She 'caught his arm for a second' but 'almost before realising it he was gone'. She was 'sure he slipped'. Her scream alerted Tyrell, who 'immediately responded and reported to the bridge'. It was 5 a.m.: 'The ship was immediately turned round, two lighted life buoys thrown overboard, emergency boats manned, officers and men stationed to keep a lookout …' *Majestic* steamed 1½ miles to the westward of the buoys and circled slowly for an hour, but he could not be found. There was a 'strong wind … accompanied by heavy rain and rough sea'.

In his memoirs, Dr Beaumont wrote that 'the big majority of travellers behave well', but a ship's officer had to '*officially* [original emphasis] – shut his eyes and ears to much that goes on. Only in flagrant cases, or where a direct complaint has been made, does he step in …' He recalled 'young fellows … dancing indecently with bobbed flappers; all hilarious with drink'; 'an all-night orgy by a party of six'; and passengers 'using empty staterooms and even [life] boats during night hours for immoral purposes'. He disapproved of the dancing. He thought 'young "modern" men, perchance even college ones, are the chief offenders, ably supported by "modern" flappers …' He was 'all in favour of the exuberance of youth' but critical of the 'restlessness, the insatiable thirst for excitement, the lack of discipline and the absence of respect for seniors – to say nothing of parents'. He asked: 'Are these going to be the fathers and mothers of the next generation: if so, what is it all going to end in?'

Majestic encountered the sea's fury. On 31 March 1927 she arrived in New York twenty-four hours late after a stormy crossing, and at times she had slowed down to as little as 7 knots. Passengers told the press that it 'was one of the roughest crossings they had ever made'. Two 3-ton derrick beams had been wrenched loose, after the ship was hit by a particularly strong wave. One of them smashed a ventilator and carried away the railing on one of the forward deckhouses. Then there were troubles with crewmen bringing illicit alcohol on board or generally misbehaving. On 18 April 1927, 'six bottles of stout and two bottles of ale brought on board at Southampton contrary to regulations' and 'two bottles of whisky' were discovered and 'thrown overboard' in the presence of the offending crewmen. On the evening of 4 October 1927, Fifth Electrician Pratt was walking up the 'stairs from the mooring deck to the forward well deck' to replace a broken light over the gangway. He caught up to Able Seaman Lanham, who refused to let him pass, declaring: 'I'll let no bastard in brass buttons pass me.' He struck Pratt violently, leaving him with two black eyes.

And so 1927 came to an end. *Majestic* returned to Southampton on 30 December 1927. Her passenger carryings worked out at an average of 1,304 passengers per crossing in 1927, one of the highest she ever achieved. White Star were busy making plans for improvements in her passenger accommodation. Ten days before she returned to Southampton, the Board of Trade was being consulted about a plan to improve third-class passenger facilities: a temporary stewards' mess room on F-deck was going to be converted into a third-class dining saloon. (A watertight door needed to be cut in a bulkhead to provide communication with the smoke and general rooms and their permission was required. The hinged watertight door, from Mechan & Co., would be 6ft 6in high and 3ft 6in wide.) Following an extensive refit early in 1928, her gross tonnage rose to 56,621 tons.

Robert Hume had a long and successful career with the White Star Line. Born in Kirkcudbright, Scotland, in 1873, he served as an officer on ships including White Star's first *Majestic*; *Olympic* and *Adriatic*. He transferred from *Olympic* to *Homeric*, serving from May 1922 to October 1924; *Majestic* in November and December 1924; and *Medic* from April 1925. From November 1925, he served as Staff Captain (or Assistant Commander) of *Majestic*; from April 1926, he served in the same position on *Olympic*; and from December 1927 to November 1928 again on *Majestic*. He served, briefly, as *Majestic*'s commander in August and September 1928, then went on to command a succession of ships including *Cedric*, *Doric*, *Adriatic*, *Megantic* and *Laurentic*. He retired in March 1933. Here, he looks down from *Majestic*'s starboard bridge wing. Below him, to the left, was an emergency boat (the uppermost lifeboat visible in the photo) and two lifeboats beneath (the largest of which was almost 31ft long, over 10ft wide and over 4ft deep). (David Hume Elkington collection)

Among the passengers travelling on *Majestic* at this time were 10-year-old Eta Progrebiesky and her mother Shandel, who made a voyage around 1928. Due to immigration restrictions, their hopes of a new life, free from the persecution that they had experienced in Russia, had been dashed for six years, during which time they had lived in Romania. They were fortunate to be able to travel second class, thanks to a relative in the United States who had worked hard to earn the money for their passage. Eta recalled that since neither she nor her mother could speak English, they had great difficulty ordering food – leading to one steward in the dining saloon starting to serve them the entire menu. She enjoyed exploring the ship's endless decks and rooms, and became fascinated by the ship's lifts. One of the lift operators found her a chair, where she sat happily riding up and down the decks. In later years she would have fond memories of the 'beautiful ship' and recall how thrilled they had been to sail on her. As *Majestic* came into New York they were both on deck to see the Statue of Liberty. Shandel explained to her daughter the concept of freedom represented by the statue. The United States was their new country, providing a life of freedom and security. Eta was to appreciate these qualities for her entire life.

Captain Metcalfe retired in September 1928 due to ill health. *Majestic*'s Assistant Commander Robert Hume took command temporarily for the 5 September 1928 westbound departure. Metcalfe's permanent replacement was Captain William Marshall, who joined the ship that same month after serving on *Olympic* from 1925. He was only in command for a few voyages before *Majestic* suffered significant damage. She departed Southampton on 9 January 1929. By the afternoon of 14 January 1929 *Majestic* had run into moderate westerly gales and head seas. From 1.16 p.m. speed was reduced gradually. Two hours later, the ship's turbines were making seventy-five revolutions, or about 8 knots; by that time, the gale had worsened to force nine.[5] It was at 3.20 p.m. that an enormous wave broke over the ship's bow, which *Majestic*'s chief officer described as 'the piling up of successive seas'. The force was enough to 'stove in' the number 1 hatch covers and yet the foredeck was about 44ft above the load water line. The mass of water poured down the hatchway, causing extensive flooding throughout the ship's forward passenger decks:

> The second sea flooded the well abaft the forward bridge space and the back wash up the starboard alleyway of that space killed a third class cook, Leon Ardi Fidini, his body being recovered later as it was washed aft.
>
> The vessel was further eased down and temporary covers were fitted to the hatch, while the passengers and crew were moved to dry quarters aft …

A survey of the damage immediately after the accident showed that the hatch side coamings had sprung at the top, the centre steel fore and after had collapsed, the hatch beams falling with it, and that the hinge pins on the heavy steel covers had sheared and the covers themselves forced down through the hatchway, breaking through the hatch below on E deck and falling on a motor car stowed on F deck hatchway, crushed it down to a height of 2 feet.

Water surged aft through the E-deck third-class promenade area, down the staircase and along the working alleyway on G-deck; the accommodation on G, H and J-decks was flooded (as much as 6ft deep on J-Kdeck). (see page 108) *Majestic* reached New York on 16 January 1929, bringing in 1,171 passengers.

Key Deck Designations		
German Plans, 1921	**As completed, 1922**	**As refitted, 1929**
Bootsdeck	A-deck	Boat deck (Sun Deck)
Oberes Promenadendeck	B-deck	Promenade Deck
Unteres Promenadendeck	C-deck	A-deck
Bruecken Deck	D-deck	B-deck
I Deck	E-deck	C-deck
II Deck	F-deck	D-deck
III Deck	G-deck	E-deck
IV Deck	H-deck	F-deck
V Deck	I-deck	G-deck

Majestic saw numerous changes to her deck designations: her first designations used during design and construction, as *Bismarck*; the second when she was completed as *Majestic*; and the third when she was refitted at the end of the 1920s. (These changes do not even take into account her service as *Caledonia*). (Author's collection)

The new NDL liner *Bremen* wrested the Blue Riband from *Mauretania* in 1929, after twenty-two years, which also set *Majestic* back in how she ranked in speed. One of White Star's officials argued: 'The *Majestic* has never been driven to her limit of speed on a regular run. We find that extreme speed means added vibration, which passengers do not find agreeable … The schedule is regulated to an unvariable crossing time of less than six days.' She carried 34,894 passengers in 1929, slightly down on previous years and slightly below *Berengaria*'s total but higher than *Aquitania*.

Plenty of changes happened as *Majestic* entered 1930: Captain Marshall became ill in March 1930. Captain F.A. Frank (from *Megantic*) was recorded both as *Majestic*'s assistant commander and commander early in April 1930, before Captain E.L. Trant took command on 15 April 1930. In turn, Trant was replaced by *Olympic*'s commander Eustace R. White on 13 June 1930. (Captain Marshall passed away on 29 May 1930.) On a happier note, Chief Engineer Wolff left the ship after eight years to enjoy a well-earned retirement.

Unfortunately, as competition from newer ships increased on the North Atlantic, financial strains mounted within Kylsant's shipping empire. *Oceanic*'s construction was effectively cancelled due to lack of funds, even if it was only officially 'delayed' (Kylsant's explanation was that the design of her propulsion system needed to be considered further). In May 1930 the Ordinary General Meeting of the White Star Line was held. Lord Kylsant presided. He mentioned that the passenger carryings in all classes by *Majestic*, *Olympic* and *Homeric* in 1929 had been 'fairly well maintained'. He noted that competition on the Atlantic was intensifying, but was optimistic about the future and America's reviving prosperity: 'During the coming months, when the volume of travel across the Atlantic is usually at its height, I hope that we may see indications of renewed activity, and that the White Star Line, with its fine vessels and increased efficiency, will continue to obtain its full share of traffic in the North Atlantic trade, in which it has been prominent for nearly sixty years.' His confidence in the future was misplaced.

On 13 December 1930, *Majestic* left New York with 146 first-, 165 second- and 495 third-class passengers. The influence of new competition and worsening economic conditions was already apparent: 1930 was the last calendar year in which *Majestic* made an overall net profit, down substantially from 1929. (Author's collection)

AN EMPTYING OCEAN

White Star were acutely aware of rising competition from newer liners such as the French Line's *Ile de France* (1927) and NDL's *Bremen* (1929) and *Europa* (1930). The sad reality as 1931 dawned was that passenger numbers were falling and many of the passengers who did travel were choosing newer ships. Since the late 1920s, White Star had been taking all sorts of small measures to try and keep *Majestic* competitive. In September 1929 approval was given for the long tables in the second-class dining saloon to be replaced by smaller individual tables for two and four people. Tourist third cabin staterooms were remodelled and new wardrobes installed, while additional cane furniture was brought aboard for third-class areas. Handrails were fitted to the third-class stairways. One month later, linoleum was renewed in the first- and second-class companionways. In 1930 a miniature golf course was installed, while in October 1930 a plan was approved to improve the ventilation of tourist third cabins, 'in view of the importance of the tourist traffic'. Thirty-five new baths were installed in first class, replacing the ageing originals. Bedside switches were fitted in the second-class cabins on D-deck. New private bathrooms were installed. In April 1931 approval was given for a portable dance floor to be installed in the first-class restaurant, for use after 11.30 p.m. That July, it was reported that it covered 425 sq ft, and included 236,940 pieces of Austrian oak, walnut, mahogany, maple, and rosewood 'glued and hydraulically compressed to a canvas backing'. Furnishings were renewed and improved, and every detail upgraded to attract passengers.

They had to spend money to keep *Majestic* in good running order. She continued to experience minor fires, typically attributed to her wiring, including a 'slight fire' and 'minor damage' in one of the first-class staterooms at Southampton on 17 January 1930. (Her sister *Leviathan* had been completely rewired at enormous expense after the war.) Generally her machinery was perfectly sound and her engines continued to perform well. However, a few signs of age were appearing that required attention – loose rivets and fractures in the hull plating were noted in February 1931, aft on B and C-deck. There was a 10in portside fracture, and one of 16in on the starboard side. In March 1931 creaking was reported in rooms amidships on B, C and D-deck; after consultation with Harland & Wolff, B-deck was stiffened with the installation of a new girder underneath. Extra stanchions were fitted. That solved the problem, since the creaking had been attributed to structural weakness. Two slight fractures forward on C-deck required fitting with doubling plates, while some welding was required for the gangway doors near the D-deck mailroom. In July 1931 small fractures were discovered 'at the top of the outer plate of the sheer strake' near the forward expansion joint, port and starboard, which required repairs, a little way forward of the stiffening completed in 1925. Two months later permanent repairs were approved, consisting of new high-tensile steel plating being riveted to the hull, extending 9ft forward and aft of the expansion joint on both sides of the ship.

Majestic's schedule included a number of cruises in 1931. White Star were keen to bring in revenue wherever they could. When she arrived at Halifax in early August 1931, the *Halifax Herald* wrote that the world's largest liner docked with 'perfect ease'. When it was time to depart, two passengers nearly missed it:

> Just as the gangway was hauled away a taxi tore up to the dock with two passengers of the *Majestic* who had misjudged the time of departure. Both were women passengers, a mother and daughter, the mother being quite an elderly lady. Consternation reigned but it was quickly dealt with when Col. A.N. Jones, agent for the White Star Line, summoned one of the tugs which was guiding the *Majestic* from the pier and both of the tardy passengers were put on board the tug and rushed to the side of the great liner which by that time had reached mid-stream and was headed out to sea.[1]

On 1 September 1931, the British press reported on a monkey (called 'Jenny') who had stowed away on *Majestic*: 'Her crimes include stowing away, stealing fruit and attacking an officer with intent to do him bodily harm. Where Jenny came from is a mystery, but it is assumed that she boarded the *Majestic* from an oiler when the big ship was being fuelled in New York prior to making a week end cruise.' She climbed to the bridge 'and made her way into the ventilating system of the officers' quarters. Here she was happy.' She was caught stealing grapes from the captain's stateroom and, finally, apprehended: 'She will probably be handed over to the Southampton zoo …'

Captain Eustace R. White was replaced by Captain Edgar L. Trant at the end of 1931. With the financial position worsening

dramatically, the White Star Line's tenth and final £104,000 instalment due on the *Majestic* had not been paid as scheduled in April 1931. They sought an extension from the British government, who approved it. Cunard felt that the White Star Line had broken the terms of the 1921 agreement. As it turned out, White Star paid the final instalment (with an additional £2,878 2*s* 6*d* in interest) on 2 December 1931. They were trying to achieve the same 'successful' economies Cunard had achieved with *Berengaria*. On 31 July 1931, G.A. Howe wrote from the accountants' department to his Cunard colleague H.B. Evans: 'we are particularly anxious … to get the disbursements of the *Majestic* down to rock bottom at once …' These efforts reflected the worsening financial position. Lord Kylsant was imprisoned in September 1931 for publishing misleading information in the 1928 Royal Mail prospectus. In June 1932, by court order, the break-up of the Royal Mail group began and the White Star Line became an independent entity again.[2] Sadly, the company continued to weaken and by the end of 1933 the boards of Cunard and the White Star Line were meeting to seal a merger of the two long-time rivals.[3]

In August 1932 Cunard and White Star ended their 'pooling on profits' between the *Berengaria* and *Majestic*. According to a newspaper report, 'for the last year or more the latter company [Cunard] has been dissatisfied with the agreement [on profit sharing] on the ground that their ship, *Berengaria*, had earned more than the *Majestic* …' For instance, in the June quarter of 1931 Cunard owed White Star £14,109 for *Berengaria*'s voyages 132–136, yet White Star owed Cunard £11,827 for *Majestic*'s voyages 129–133. During the September quarter, Cunard owed White Star more than twice as much as White Star owed to them. As of 18 March 1932, Cunard were recorded as owing White Star £63,193.

Captain Trant was named as White Star's new commodore early in August 1932, but *Majestic* did not end 1932 on the best of notes. She suffered some bad damage in heavy weather.

Majestic takes on oil fuel *c.*1932. The men working on the oiler alongside her are overseeing fuelling through one of several 'oiling doors' in the side of the hull, behind which was an 'oil filling station'. (*Süddeutsche Zeitung* Photo/ Alamy Stock Photo)

According to a reporter from the *New York Times*, she arrived in port 'with her decks strewn with debris from [the] blow of waves'. One particularly bad wave, estimated at 45ft high and 1,500 tons in weight, broke over the bow at 1.30 p.m. on the first Friday out of port, 700 miles from Cherbourg. Able Seaman J.H. Johnston was caught by the wave and dashed against the steel bulkhead near the crew's galley. He was found dead fifteen minutes later (towards the end of the voyage the passengers collected $250 for Johnston's widow, son and daughter in Portsmouth). Two galley cooks had a lucky escape when the sea tore off the door, ripped open the thick steel bulkhead and lifted the deck by 1ft. The lookouts' quarters, by the galley on the starboard side, were flooded by the wave. 'The wave was so high that it broke over the sun deck 60ft above the waterline, smashing rails and a heavy wooden door and twelve windows on the starboard side of the promenade deck 10ft below', wrote an observer. Many of the deck fittings were damaged or washed away, and Captain Trant told reporters that at times the ship had slowed to 7 knots, making her a day late. More than 1,000 passengers were on board, and some spoke to the press. They said: 'The ship withstood the shock admirably and, after a violent shudder, was quite easy in the succession of lesser seas which followed.' Several were upset that their clothing had been damaged, as a result of the baggage hold flooding.

On 15 February 1933, the *Western Mail* reported that 3 tons of paint had been used during *Majestic*'s annual overhaul: 'It took fifty skilled workmen twenty-four hours' continuous work to paint the ship's bottom.' Two of her propeller shafts were withdrawn for 'overhaul and inspection' and *Majestic* received two new propellers weighing over 15 tons each, which 'will further maintain the *Majestic*'s reputation for steady speed in all weathers …' Her running mate *Olympic* was, meanwhile, nearing the end of an extensive refit, but the economic climate was no better.

By the spring of 1933, *Majestic*'s losses were causing mounting concern. In an article on 26 March 1933, a passenger agent said: 'The British lines cannot afford to continue losing money much longer. The *Majestic* arrived on Wednesday with 240 passengers all told, and sailed again yesterday with a total list of 300. This means a loss of $75,000 on the round voyage.' Whether or not the figures were correct, certainly the situation was bad and she was racking up heavy losses. Times were tough for charities, too. The *Belfast Telegraph* reported the Star Ball would be held on board at Southampton on 12 May 1933: 'This ball is in aid of the Sunshine Homes for the Blind babies educated by the National Institute for the Blind. The swimming pool … will be filled with water from the Atlantic before reaching Southampton, so that the guests at the ball will be able to bathe during the evening …'

Guests were going to spend the night on board and enjoy breakfast the next morning. Early in June 1933, the White Star Line announced that, in addition to the indoor first-class swimming pools on *Olympic* and *Majestic*, outdoor pools had been installed on the *Majestic* for tourist and third-class passengers. 'Similar pools will be installed on the *Olympic* on her next visit to Southampton,' the *New York Times* recorded. Everything was being done to give the impression that the ships were fully up to date.

'The *Majestic* Leaving Southampton for New York.' This impressive image was published in the October 1934 issue of *White Star Magazine*. The publication ran from September 1923 through October 1934 and ceased as a result of the Cunard White Star merger. (*White Star Magazine*, 1934/Daniel Klistorner collection)

A night-time view of *Majestic* in the dry dock. (Riccardo Mancioli Archive & Historical/Alamy Stock Photo)

On 19 January 1934, *Majestic* entered the new King George V graving dock at Southampton. She was a day late because of high winds the previous day. The dock had been opened officially by the King in July 1933, but *Majestic* was reportedly the first civilian ship to use it. *The Sphere* wrote: 'the task of edging this 100-foot-wide liner into a space allowing only a small clearance on either side was one of extreme delicacy, and it was nearly an hour before the eight attendant tugs could get her into the entrance way. The dock holds 260,000 tons of water and yet can be pumped dry in four hours. It is 1,200 feet long, 135 to 165 feet wide and 45 to 48½ feet deep, and is largely constructed of concrete …' (*Süddeutsche Zeitung* Photo/Alamy Stock Photo)

The Cunard–White Star merger took effect on 1 July 1934. It was reported that the express service from Southampton to New York would be 'maintained by the *Berengaria*, *Majestic*, *Aquitania* and *Olympic*, the *Homeric* being engaged in cruising from British ports, and the *Mauretania* cruising from New York to the West Indies'. The merger had secured a strong British company positioned to take on foreign rivals, but it found itself with more ships than it needed and the end of the line was coming into view for most of their express ships.

Several months after the merger, *Majestic* grounded 'on the mud off the West Brambles Buoy' as she returned to Southampton. The *Nottingham Evening Post* reported on 12 September 1934 that she 'was going practically dead slow, and was only on the mud for about a quarter of an hour. She refloated under her own power, and then anchored off Cowes for more than an hour to wait for the tide.' Passengers were not alarmed: 'nothing was felt except that they realised that the engines had stopped', by one account. She did not dock until 1 a.m. (three hours after the scheduled time).

One of the major events of *Majestic*'s career occurred on 4 October 1934, a day out of Cherbourg. A huge wave crashed over the ship's port bow and glass from four of the heavy bridge windows shattered, knocking Captain Trant backwards on to the deck and leaving him with head injuries. Second Officer H. McGill was more fortunate, escaping with only minor cuts. Meanwhile, one of the ship's forward cabins was also flooded. Trant was taken to the ship's hospital, and Assistant Commander Frederick Burd took over temporarily; *Majestic* was battered by heavy seas as the voyage wore on and she docked a day late. (Trant was admitted to hospital in New York, returning home as a passenger on *Olympic* early in December 1934 and then retiring.) Captain Robert B. Irving took over *Majestic* at a time when the worst of the Depression was easing. *Majestic*'s net losses peaked in 1933 and her financial results were already improving.

Irving was in command when *Majestic* was delayed arriving in New York, early in January 1935. She sat in the outer harbour for the best part of two days because it was too foggy to navigate her into port safely. Once visibility improved to ¾ mile, Irving decided to proceed and they soon got to Quarantine. Ashore, workers had been making preparations so she could sail on time for the return crossing. Irving, standing in the middle of his large stateroom 'with a pipe in his mouth', spoke to reporters and said he was 'not going to "give you a lot of honey about standing on the bridge sixty hours at a stretch"'. Passengers 'went on as usual; they played cards, danced, went to the movies, looked at the fog and strolled about the decks. As far as I know they had a good time. And they had forty-eight hours free on the ship.'

Majestic was three days late when she arrived in New York on 1 March 1935, having been held for twenty-four hours at Southampton in stormy weather. Irving recalled for reporters: 'We ran into a series of gales with high confused seas from the north-west, which reached the peak … when we had a whole gale blowing at hurricane force, with very high seas, and we reduced the speed to seven knots for several hours.' No damage was reported to the ship or her 354 passengers.

By April 1935, both *Mauretania* and *Olympic* had been withdrawn from service, but passenger traffic was improving significantly: late in June 1935, *Majestic* contributed to a record 18,000 tourists leaving New York in twelve hours on several liners. (A giant iceberg that had been reported 'in the direct path of transatlantic liners at the height of this summer's tourist season … finally melted away' by 23 July 1935.) Section 'S' of *Majestic*'s third-class accommodation – which had not been in use for several years – was reopened due to a rising number of passengers. Several crewmen's rooms were converted into passenger accommodation as well. A few complaints were received from tourist-class passengers around the same time, speaking of 'uncomfortable beds', and so a number were replaced by Marshall mattresses. The improvement in passenger traffic belied a gloomy mood for former White Star officers now serving the new company, who spoke to the *New York Times*. They thought *Olympic* would be 'scrapped soon'. *Homeric* was reported to follow her and *Majestic* was 'understood' to be scheduled to be 'taken out of service when the *Queen Mary*' went into service in summer 1936: 'the veterans grieve because it looks as if the old flag they have worn on their caps and buttons for so many years is soon to be sunk for all time'.

On her round trip leaving Southampton on 21 August and returning on 3 September 1935, *Majestic*'s passenger numbers rose to 1,855 – an average of more than 900 on each crossing and a better performance than both *Aquitania* and *Berengaria*. She recorded a gross profit of almost £19,000 with a net profit of £4,244. She marked the completion of the westbound leg of her 200th round trip when she arrived in New York on 10 September 1935: 'The liner came in with several of her portholes broken by stormy seas and with salt encrusted on her three towering stacks where the wind had carried huge waves.' Her officers said the winds 'reached hurricane force'.

On 3 November 1935, the *New York Times* reported that the *Berengaria* was to be retired as soon as the *Queen Mary* entered service, leaving *Aquitania* and *Majestic* operating the express service with the new liner: 'Presumably the *Berengaria* will share the fate of the *Mauretania* and *Olympic*, both of which are being scrapped after long and honourable service on the Atlantic.' It was not to be. When the next sailing schedule was published in New York towards the end of November 1935, *Majestic* was not shown after her 20 February 1936 departure. The westbound schedule released at Southampton on 9 December 1935 merely confirmed the situation. Cunard White Star's general passenger traffic manager in New York, H.P. Borer, had no definitive information about her fate, but 'believed the *Majestic* would be held in reserve to operate

in the transatlantic service if traffic developed sufficiently to warrant her operation or for long cruise service'. The *Liverpool Echo* noted *Majestic* 'does not appear in the sailings after 13 February' 1936 and the *Belfast Telegraph* reported 'it is almost certain' she would be scrapped.

While there was speculation that the apparent change had been because *Berengaria* was proving more popular, *Majestic*'s passenger carryings were rising strongly by 1935. She carried 18,051 passengers in 1932 and 13,573 in 1933, rising to 15,465 in 1934. In 1935 she carried 19,586 passengers – her best since 1930 – at an average of 632 per crossing, according to the North Atlantic Passenger Conference. Perhaps the recollection that *Berengaria* had earned more than *Majestic* prior to the 'profit pool' being terminated contributed to the decision, since both ships appeared about equal in the popularity stakes. Certainly, *Majestic*'s profits were still lower than *Berengaria* in both 1934 and 1935. (In hindsight, *Berengaria*'s subsequent electrical problems and her enforced withdrawal from service in 1938 raises the question as to whether it might have been better to retain the younger *Majestic*.)

This aerial view of *Majestic* in the 1930s showed off her sleek profile to great effect. The tugboats look tiny in comparison. (Author's collection)

Majestic returned to New York at the start of January 1936 after a successful New Year's cruise with 1,501 passengers. The *New York Times* reported: 'Five cruising steamships returned yesterday from Bermuda, Nassau and the West Indies with 4,829 tourists.' Captain Gibbons was in command as *Majestic* made her first round voyage of 1936. John Havers was fortunate to visit her that January and he later recalled: 'She seemed in perfect condition as far as the accommodation went. Certainly not fit for the scrappers … This ship … was all her name implied.' He thought she was magnificent:

The huge entrance hall between the palm court and the lounge was a sight on its own. Two decks high, a wide gentle staircase leading to a balcony, wrought iron gates led into the lounge with pictures of the King and Queen on either side of the gates. The lounge itself was twenty-six feet high, with a wrought glass dome of 3,600sq.ft. It was full of panelling, paintings, lovely furniture and drapes; full of dignity. Forward of the lounge was the reading and writing room and aft of the main entrance hall was the palm court, joined by a short staircase to the á la carte restaurant. [The] last room on the promenade deck was the card room. The restaurant seated 133 and was an alternative to the saloon. It was beautifully designed with tall Ionic pillars and had a view through the palm court. There were 748 chair positions on the promenade deck … The dining saloon on D-deck seated 678 people. Soaring columns went right round the room, supporting a beautifully decorated dome. With reddish furniture and table lights, cream columns, green railings between the columns on the deck above, where the orchestra played, made this one of the finest rooms I have seen afloat. Perhaps surpassed by the sheer grandeur of the *Normandie*

but much more dignified … The swimming bath was also three decks high, from the bath bottom to the tops of its dozen or more giant fluted pillars. A truly Roman style bath – sheer grandeur and quite breathtaking.[4]

The 'Magic-Stick' had lost none of her touch! She entered New York later in January 1936 'with colours at half mast' as a mark of respect to the late King George V and the press recalled his late Majesty's Royal visit fourteen years earlier. Captain Gibbons was replaced by Captain Peter Vaughan for the 13 February 1936 Southampton departure. After arriving in New York for the final time on 19 February 1936, some of her officers spoke to the *New York Times*. They feared that *Majestic* was going to be scrapped and they 'said that the only thing wrong with the ship was that she had the wrong colour funnels' – a clear reference to her status as one of White Star's proudest ships. There was a perception that the new company, with Cunard interests controlling the majority, was biased against White Star's old vessels.

By the time of her final round trip, the number of crew that she carried had declined to 687. At her peak in the 1920s, her crew had numbered between 1,050 and 1,100. There were many people who had a good word to say about her, including Captain Vaughan, who recalled that he had originally joined her as a first officer under Captain Sir Bertram Hayes. She was 'nine years younger and a full knot-and-a-half faster than the *Berengaria*, and a splendid heavy weather ship, but not quite so good as the *Olympic* was, according to the Captains who have commanded both'. It made it all the more sad that she was coming to the end of her Atlantic service. Atlantic veterans said that 'after the scrapping of the *Olympic*, recognised as one of the finest steamships afloat, there were no surprises left'.

Majestic (background) and *Queen Mary* (foreground) present an impressive sight in this view of Southampton on 27 May 1936. (The smaller four-funnel liner appears to be the Union Castle Line's *Winchester Castle*.) *Queen Mary* was significantly larger and represented a generation of progress in shipbuilding: technology had advanced to the point where, by the early 1930s, it was possible for two larger express ships to run the New York service instead of three. However, her running mate *Queen Elizabeth* would not be completed for several years. (Trinity Mirror/Mirrorpix/Alamy Stock Photo)

And so *Majestic*'s service came to an end after completing her 207th eastbound crossing. She was laid up. In April 1936, Cunard White Star received a letter from Messrs McGregor, Gow & Holland, advising them that they were 'approaching the various shipbreakers to see if they would be interested'. Cunard White Star responded that 'when any of them desire to inspect [*Majestic*] we will arrange the necessary facilities'. They confirmed she could 'be run at speeds from 14 to 18 knots with the oil consumption varying' from 340 to 440 tons per day: 'These speeds would necessitate using two sections of boilers.' Early in May 1936, they made enquiries as to whether the British government had any use for her, but the Admiralty indicated they did not. Later that month, *Majestic* was sold for scrapping to Thomas Ward's. Many fittings were sold at auction in June 1936. On 16 June 1936, Cunard White Star's Board minutes recorded that the whole of the £115,100 purchase price for the *Majestic* had been handed over and the liner had been formally delivered the previous day. At the beginning of August 1936 it was reported that she would take *Olympic*'s place at Jarrow by 6 September 1936. In a remarkable turnaround, however, the Admiralty advised that they needed the ship. Cunard White Star noted on 25 August 1936:

The Admiralty advise that an urgent need has recently arisen for additional depot accommodation in the United Kingdom for the training of boys for the Royal Navy and it is desired to utilise the *Majestic* for this purpose … In view of the national urgency, the company has agreed to waive the clause in the contract calling for the vessel to be broken up forthwith and the Admiralty has undertaken that on the completion of this temporary service the *Majestic* will be demolished. The *Majestic* is being transferred by Messrs Ward to the Admiralty as from September 1st 1936.

Majestic was set for a new career!

Majestic's plush fittings were listed for sale. Buyers had plenty of items to choose from. Fittings from the 'bridge deck' alone (apparently the bridge and officers' quarters) included 'ships' telegraph'; 'ships' course indicator'; 'ships' compass and binnacle stand'; 'ships' steering wheel 3'3"'; 'teak flag locker, 5' long'; 'bridge teak panelling'; 'steering indicator'; 'four lifebuoys'; 'teak gratings'; 'bridge teak handrailings'; 'walnut wardrobe …'; 'oak bookcase and writing desk, 2'7"' (two); '3 candle electric lamp'; 'porcelain wash basin and mirror'; and 'white enamelled panelled bed' … (Author's collection)

An unused railway ticket voucher for buyers travelling to see *Majestic* at Southampton. They had to present the voucher when they booked their train ticket in order to obtain a reduced fare. (Author's collection)

Eight years after she was launched in Germany as *Bismarck*, the new ship is registered in Britain under the name *Majestic*. (United Kingdom National Archives)

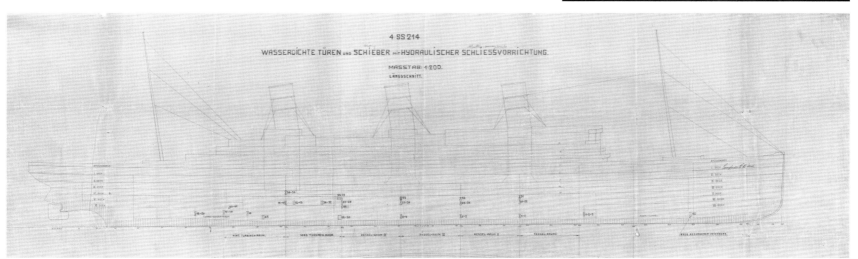

Blohm & Voss plan showing the watertight doors that were closed hydraulically. There were forty-one hydraulically closed watertight doors in total and a number of others that were closed manually. (The foremost boiler room was 'Kessel Raum I': the boiler rooms were numbered from the bow. The turbine engine rooms were not numbered but designated as 'Vord. Turbinen-Raum' and 'Hint. Turbinen-Raum'.)(United Kingdom National Archives)

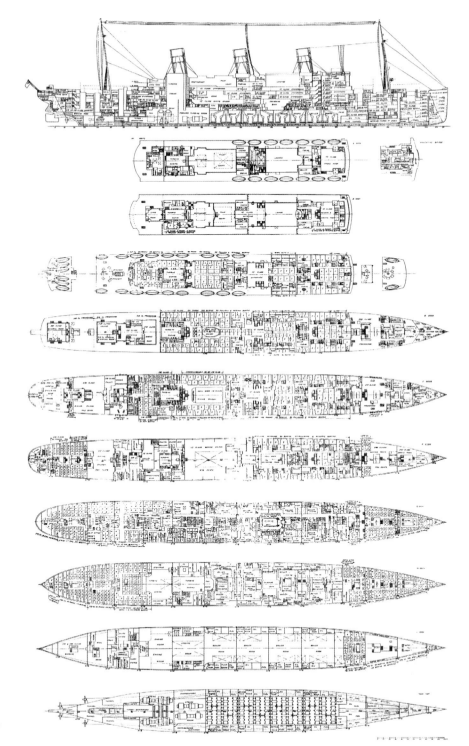

These *Majestic* general arrangement plans give a good idea of the ship's layout and configuration when she entered service in 1922. (*The Shipbuilder*/J. Kent Layton collection)

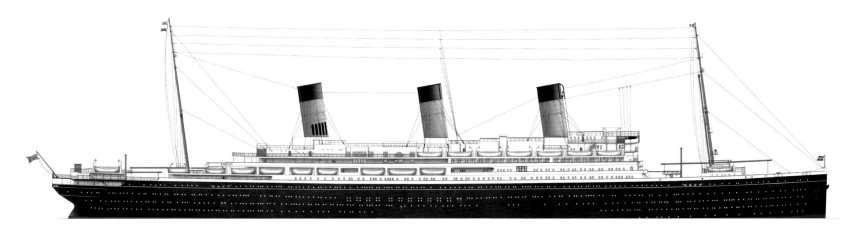

This coloured rigging plan of *Majestic* illustrates her profile well: two towering masts and three imposing funnels. (Lionel Codus © 2011)

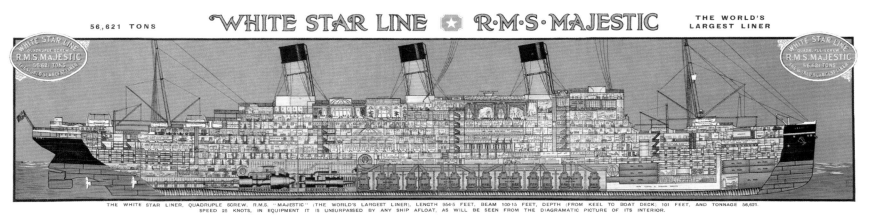

WHITE STAR LINE ☆ R·M·S·MAJESTIC

THE WORLD'S
LARGEST LINER

WHITE STAR LINE
R.M.S. MAJESTIC
QUADRUPLE SCREW
56,621 TONS
THE WORLD'S LARGEST LINER

WHITE STAR LINE
R.M.S. MAJESTIC
QUADRUPLE SCREW
56,621 TONS
THE WORLD'S LARGEST LINER

THE WHITE STAR LINER, QUADRUPLE SCREW, R.M.S. "MAJESTIC" (THE WORLD'S LARGEST LINER), LENGTH 954·5 FEET, BEAM 100·15 FEET, DEPTH (FROM KEEL TO BOAT DECK) 101 FEET, AND TONNAGE 56,621.
SPEED 25 KNOTS, IN EQUIPMENT IT IS UNSURPASSED BY ANY SHIP AFLOAT, AS WILL BE SEEN FROM THE DIAGRAMATIC PICTURE OF ITS INTERIOR.

The White Star Line's publicity department were keen to show the extent of *Majestic*'s interiors: not only the passenger accommodation, but also the crew accommodation and machinery spaces. This lovely colour cutaway was used in publicity after the 1928 refit. (Author's collection)

WHITE STAR LINE   QUADRUPLE-SCREW R.M.S. "MAJESTIC."
56,551 TONS.   AT NEW YORK.

This postcard of the *Majestic* shows her impressive profile. Her length is evident compared to the buildings in the New York skyline. (Author's collection)

WHITE STAR LINE
QUADRUPLE-SCREW R.M.S. "MAJESTIC."

Majestic's funnels towered over her hull and, in turn, she towered over the small tug boats at New York. The postcard was issued later in her career and she is described here merely as a 'quadruple screw' steamer rather than the largest ship in the world. There are a number of inaccuracies in how she was depicted, such as the openings in the ship's hull beneath the fore end of the superstructure. (Author's collection)

Clockwise from top left:
John Fry's 1923 illustration of *Majestic* shows her to be a lot narrower than she actually was. (Author's collection)

Majestic towers over the tugboats in this artist's impression. (Author's collection)

Majestic gives an impression of speed and power in this wonderful image, which shows the line's White Star emblem over the liner's bow. (Author's collection)

S.S. MAJESTIC.

DECK OF S.S. MAJESTIC

ABOARD THE MAJESTIC

ABOARD THE MAJESTIC

ABOARD "MAJESTIC"

Clockwise from above:
This wonderful view of *Majestic* was published in the mid-1920s in a colour brochure showing off the ship's luxurious accommodation. (Author's collection)

Majestic appears in all her splendour in this Wills' cigarette card. The back of the card describes her as 'one of the world's largest ships' and 'also one of the swiftest'. *Majestic*'s size was 'equivalent to that of the 132 ships which formed the Spanish Armada', according to the card. (Author's collection)

Life at sea aboard *Majestic* c.1924. Passengers are seen enjoying the fresh air from the ship's spacious decks. (The colouring in these various deck scenes is often inaccurate: a case in point is the funnel colour.)(Digital restoration © Eric K. Longo/Author's collection)

Clockwise from right:
Majestic features in this calendar for 1927 issued by the Gregory Travel Bureau in Oklahoma. (Author's collection)

Majestic ('The largest ship in the world') compared to the highest building in New York. The Woolworth Building was less than 800ft tall, meaning that *Majestic* was more than 150ft longer. (Günter Bäbler collection)

Majestic was compared with Prague Cathedral in this illustration from the mid-1920s. (Günter Bäbler collection)

QUADRUPLE-SCREW. R.M.S. "MAJESTIC". 56,551 TONS, THE WORLD'S LARGEST LINER, COMPARED WITH THE CATHEDRAL, PRAGUE.

Vierschraubendampfer „Majestic"
56,551 Tons
das größte Schiff der Welt, verglichen mit dem höchsten Gebäude in New York

Majestic appeared on a list of White Star Line sailings issued in March 1928. (Author's collection)

A dramatic illustration depicts *Majestic* as the night draws in. (Günter Bäbler collection)

Clockwise from above:

Majestic's plush *à la carte* restaurant. There was always a difference in approach between Cunard and White Star. Cunard felt that an extra-tariff restaurant in first class created two classes of first-class passenger and that some passengers using the restaurant would be inclined to look down on those dining in the saloon. Following the merger between Cunard and White Star, late in 1934 the *à la carte* restaurants on *Olympic* and *Majestic* were closed as extra tariff facilities. When *Majestic*'s fittings were auctioned off in June 1936, the fittings from the restaurant included '29 ceiling bowl lights in restaurant'; 'inlaid mahogany framed upholstered seated arm chairs'; 'mahogany framed green plush upholstered tub arm chairs'; an 'oak upright piano by Eavestaff, of London'; 'the magnificent green and vari-coloured carpet ... about 18 yards square'. (Author's collection)

The first-class dining saloon was showcased to best effect in colour. The fittings included 'white beaded wall panelling'; a 'painting by Carl Zingheim, 1872, (copy) on canvas, gilt moulding frame' about 7ft by 5ft 6in; 'approximately 1,200 square yards' of rubberine coloured flooring; and mahogany-framed tables. (Author's collection)

Majestic's swimming pool was magnificent and one of the grandest aboard any ocean liner before or since. The pool was retained when she served as HMS *Caledonia*, so it might well hold some sort of record as to the most impressive swimming pool in any British naval training facility! (Author's collection)

MAJESTIC: CRACK REPAIRS 1925

The repairs to *Majestic*'s crack damage were followed by a smaller amount of precautionary, preventative strengthening work on her sister *Leviathan*. Unfortunately, that did not stop her suffering a similar fracture several years later. J. Lyell Wilson, Assistant Chief Surveyor, American Bureau of Shipping, presented a paper about *Leviathan*'s repairs to the Society of Naval Architects and Marine Engineers (SNAME) in New York in November 1930. The paper and subsequent discussion echoed many of the problematic factors Roscoe & Little (and the Board of Trade) had identified with *Majestic* (see page 73). The position of the expansion joints was unfortunate, as Senior Ship Surveyor F.W. Daniel had noted: 'It seems evident that these [two] vessels experience considerable twisting stresses, particularly with following seas and it is significant that the fractures have occurred in way of expansion joints in the decks and sides above, and at the corners of the funnel casings. While it is not expected that the superstructure should take any material stress of the main [hull] structure, it is unfortunate, I think, that the positions of the expansion joints should coincide with the weakest portion of the strength deck.'

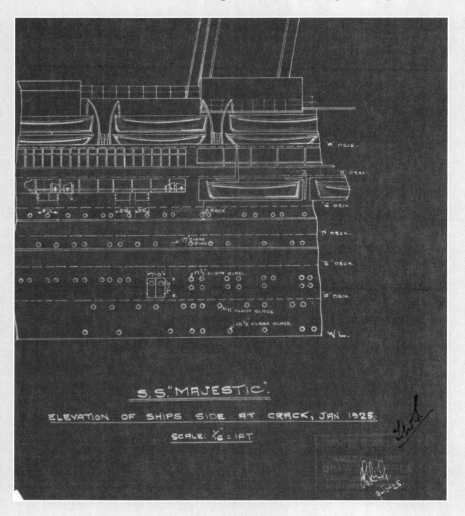

An elevation of *Majestic*'s port side abreast the second funnel, showing the visible crack in the ship's sheer strake plating, prepared by the White Star Line and American Line drawing offices early in January 1925. (United Kingdom National Archives)

One SNAME member, David Arnott, thought in fairness that 'the design of the main hull structure can be considered quite good for their day and generation'. Carl E. Petersen, a life member, pointed out that *Leviathan* had been running at a significantly greater draft than her German shipbuilders had intended. Data for eighteen round trips from February 1928 to April 1929 showed her loaded to a draft of up to $1\frac{1}{2}$ft greater than the intended maximum. All factors considered, the stress on the hull plating at the sheer strake therefore reached about 14 tons per square inch, whereas naval architects of the period normally sought to keep it to about 10 tons. To make it worse, she was being driven faster than her original designed speed: 'This increase … must have some further dynamical effect in further increasing the stresses to which the vessel's structure is subjected …'

The Board of Trade Surveyors' Office at Southampton prepared a cross section sketch of *Majestic* where the damage occurred, in December 1924. It helps to visualise where the strength deck failed and the location of the crack as it extended to the ship's side and down through the sheer strake plating. (United Kingdom National Archives)

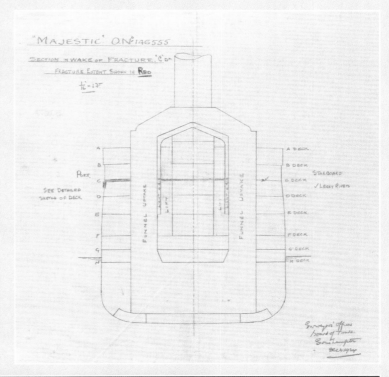

Harland & Wolff prepared a blueprint showing the work they would do to strengthen and repair C-deck. The view is from overhead, looking down at the deck: the port side is at the top. The two 'after boiler casings' represent the split uptakes beneath the second funnel and the two 'staircases' to the right represent the first-class staircase. The dotted lines running across the ship represent the beams beneath the deck that provided support. The key records that the new, additional doubling plates (to strengthen the deck) are shown in red, whereas the original plates that were being replaced are shown in yellow. Some of the replacement plates were sourced 'from stock'. The shipbuilder did a remarkable job in essentially rebuilding and redesigning a substantial portion of the strength deck amidships – doing all this in a short space of time and completing all the work on the existing ship. (United Kingdom National Archives)

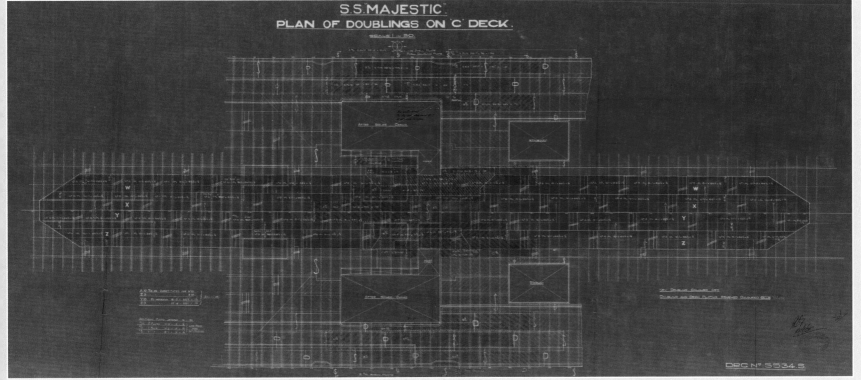

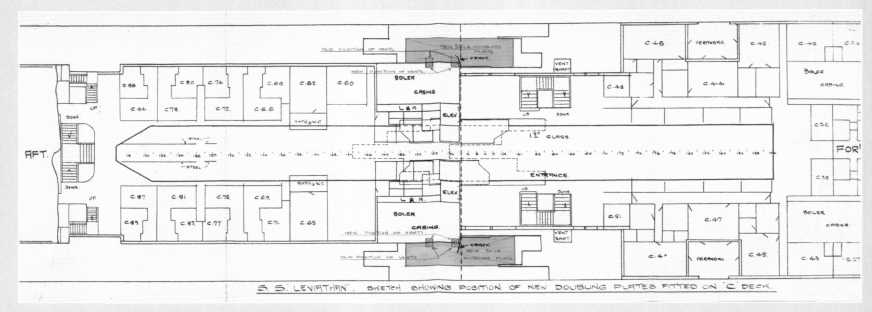

S.S. "LEVIATHAN", SKETCH SHOWING POSITION OF NEW DOUBLING PLATES FITTED ON "C" DECK.

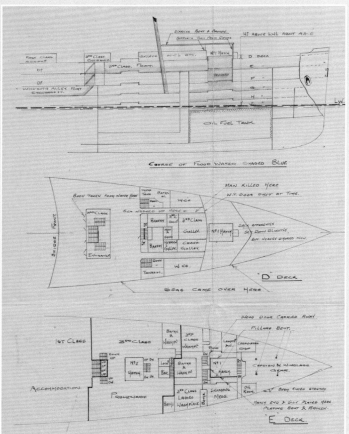

Following the damage to *Majestic*, an inspection of *Leviathan* revealed similar signs of weakness and an earlier stage of cracking. Her owners undertook some precautionary work, including moving the position of existing vents and fitting new doubling plates (shown in a light pink/red) adjacent to part of the boiler casings. However, the work was minor compared with the very substantial and extensive repairs and strengthening undertaken on *Majestic*. Predictably, the work did not prevent *Leviathan* experiencing a similar serious failure during a stormy crossing in December 1929, although it may have delayed what was inevitable. In *Leviathan*'s case, she suffered a serious fracture abreast the first funnel on the starboard side (rather than abreast the second funnel on the port side as on *Majestic*) and the crack extended slightly further down the side of the ship. However, she did not crack across the deck as *Majestic* did. She did, however, need repairs to address cracking in the region of the second funnel. (United Kingdom National Archives)

The Board of Trade produced a sketch showing the extent of the flooding and damage *Majestic* experienced in January 1929. The blue shading at the top shows just how extensive the flooding was in the fore third-class accommodation. They noted where some of the deck was 'apparently set down slightly, but heavily shored [up] now'; deck support pillars were bent and some of the 'beam knees' which connected the deck support beams to the frames at the side of the ship. (United Kingdom National Archives)

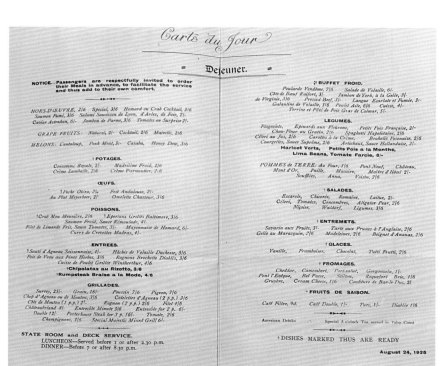

The *Carte du Jour* from *Majestic*'s *à la carte* restaurant on 24 August 1925. Customers were spoilt for choice! (Mike Poirier collection)

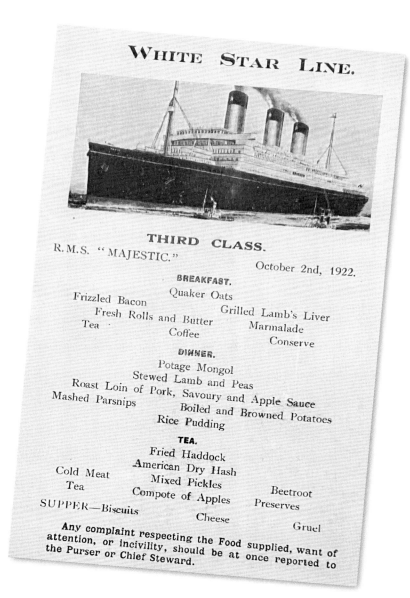

A tourist third cabin dinner menu from August 1930 and a passenger's letter written 'in middle of a rough Atlantic'. The fare was plainer, but plentiful. (Mike Poirier collection)

This third-class menu from October 1922 shows the stark differences compared with what was available in the first-class restaurant. (Mike Poirier collection)

· WHITE STAR LINE ·

R.M.S. "MAJESTIC" (Completing) 56,000 Tons.
The World's Largest Liner.
R.M.S. "HOMERIC" (Completing) 35,000 Tons.

SAILINGS.

SOUTHAMPTON—CHERBOURG—NEW YORK.
LIVERPOOL—QUEENSTOWN—NEW YORK.
LIVERPOOL—QUEENSTOWN—BOSTON.
LIVERPOOL—QUEENSTOWN—PHILADELPHIA.

LIVERPOOL—QUEBEC—MONTREAL (SUMMER SERVICE).
LIVERPOOL—HALIFAX, N.S.—PORTLAND, ME. (WINTER SERVICE).

NEW YORK—BOSTON—MEDITERRANEAN AND EGYPT
(VIA MADEIRA AND AZORES).

For Tickets and further particulars apply to—

WHITE STAR LINE:
30, James Street, LIVERPOOL
1, Cockspur Street, S.W. 1,
38, Leadenhall Street, E.C. 3, } LONDON.
Canute Road, SOUTHAMPTON.
63, Temple Row, BIRMINGHAM.

AMERICAN TRAVEL AND TRANSPORT AGENCY, 9, Rue Scribe, PARIS.
Or to any of the Offices or Agents of the Line.
Oct. 27th, 1921.—(6,000).

Majestic appeared on a White Star Line sailing advertisement issued on 27 October 1921, more than six months before she entered service. *Homeric* was listed as 'completing' as well, although she would be finished several months earlier. (Author's collection)

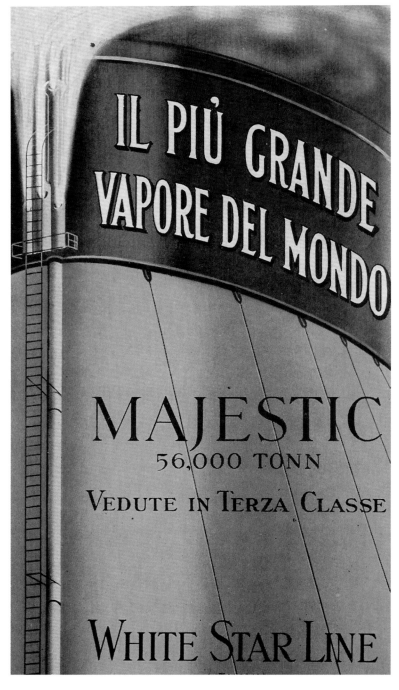

IL PIÙ GRANDE VAPORE DEL MONDO

MAJESTIC
56,000 TONN
VEDUTE IN TERZA CLASSE

WHITE STAR LINE

Majestic's funnel conveyed a sense of power in this illustration used on the front of a third-class brochure issued in Italian *c.*1922. (Author's collection)

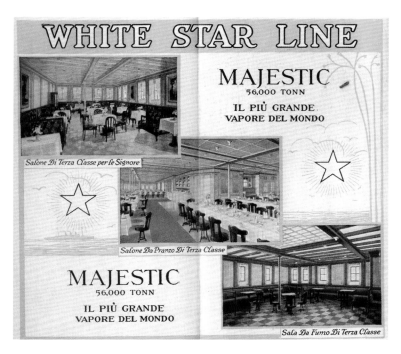

The brochure showcased the third-class accommodation, from the third-class ladies (or general) room at the top left; through to the third-class dining saloon in the middle; and the third-class smoking room at the bottom right. The text also noted her tonnage at 56,000 and described her as the largest steamer in the world. (Author's collection)

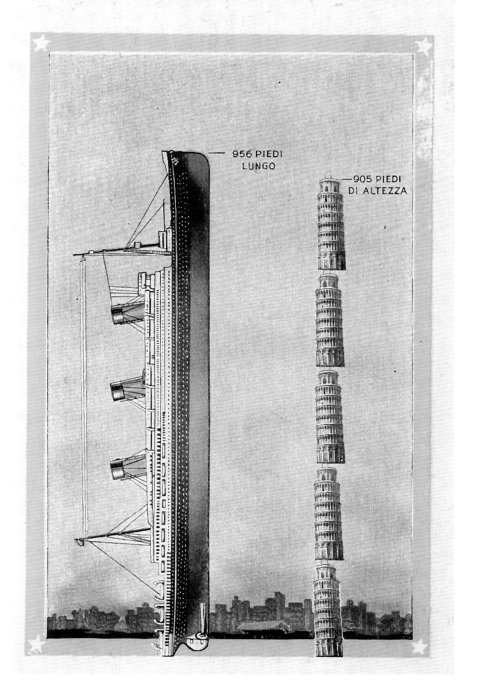

The brochure compared *Majestic*'s length to the famous (leaning) Tower of Pisa, showing that even five Towers were about 50ft shorter. (Author's collection)

THE 'NEW TOURIST CLASS'

Majestic carried first-, second- and third-class passengers when she entered service in May 1922. Later in the 1920s, she also carried tourist third cabin passengers to cater for people who wanted a better standard than third class but without the cost of second. On 1 April 1932, the White Star Line issued a colourful brochure advertising her recently implemented 'new tourist class', which was a combination of the former second class and former tourist third cabin accommodation, merged into a single 'tourist class': 'The conveniences on this magnificent steamer, the sumptuous public rooms, the broad, sunny decks, and the luxurious staterooms of the new tourist class have inspired the enthusiastic praise of thousands of discriminating travellers ...' Opening up the fold-out brochure, prospective passengers saw a magnificent illustration of *Majestic* compared against the New York skyline. The deck designations are that of her final configuration. (Author's collection)

Right: On A-deck, tourist-class passengers enjoyed ample promenade space, a new verandah and spacious staterooms. (Author's collection)

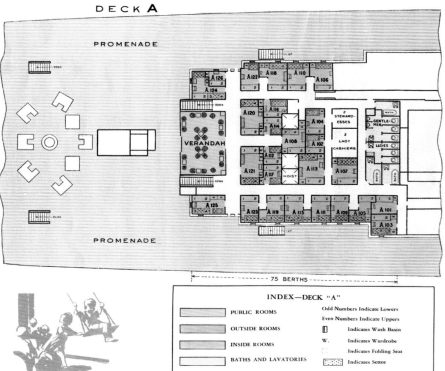

Far right: On B-deck, they had no fewer than two lounges, a reading and writing room, gymnasium, writing room and smoking room. The area around the staircases and lift included a dance floor. (The large lounge further aft was originally two rooms when the ship entered service, split into a general room/lounge and a smoke room for third-class passengers. Later, it was converted into a single large lounge for tourist third cabin passengers and, finally, became a large lounge for the combined 'new tourist class'.)(Author's collection)

S.S. MAJESTIC

World's Largest Steamer

TONS	LENGTH	BREADTH
56,621	956 feet	101 feet

WHITE STAR LINE

SUN DECK
PROMENADE DECK
A
B
C
D
E
F
G

MAJESTIC

DECK B

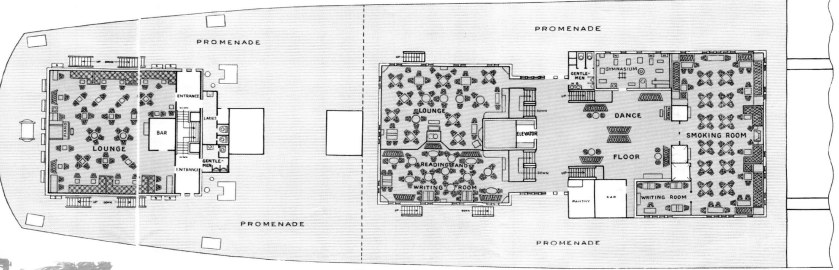

PROMENADE

PROMENADE

ENTRANCE

LADIES

BAR

LOUNGE

GENTLEMEN

ENTRANCE

PROMENADE

GENTLEMEN

GYMNASIUM

LOUNGE

DANCE

ELEVATOR

SMOKING ROOM

READING AND

FLOOR

WRITING ROOM

PANTRY

BAR

WRITING ROOM

PROMENADE

INQUIRY OFFICE ON STEAMERS—This is the business office of the ship, where letters are mailed, cables and radios despatched, and all business of the voyage conducted. Passengers may purchase return tickets or make reservations here.

SEATS AT TABLE may be reserved with the dining saloon steward immediately after sailing. Table reservations may also be made in advance when making stateroom reservations.

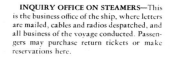

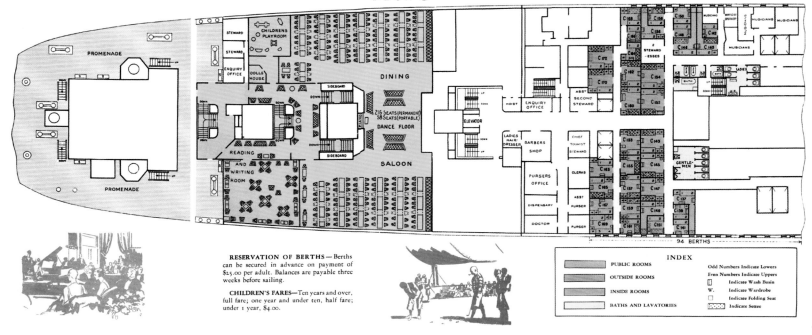

DECK C

PROMENADE

PROMENADE

STEWARD
STEWARD
ENQUIRY OFFICE
CHILDRENS PLAYROOM
DOLLS HOUSE

DINING

216 SEATS (PERMANENT)
58 SEATS (PORTABLE)

DANCE FLOOR

SALOON

READING AND WRITING ROOM

SIDEBOARD
SIDEBOARD

HOIST
ENQUIRY OFFICE
ELEVATOR
ASST SECOND STEWARD
STEWARD ESSES

LADIES HAIR DRESSER
BARBERS SHOP
CHIEF TOURIST STEWARD

PURSERS OFFICE
CLERKS

DISPENSARY
ASST PURSER

DOCTOR
PURSER

MUSICIANS
MUSICIANS
MUSICIANS
MUSICIANS

C 168 C 156 C 150
C 158
C 148 C 142
C 172
C 146 C 140
C 162 C 154
BATH
C 170
C 160 C 152
LADIES
C 153 C 143
C 155 C 145
C 165 C 157 C 147
GENTLEMEN
C 167 C 159 C 149
C 137
C 169 C 161 C 151
C 139
C 141

94 BERTHS

RESERVATION OF BERTHS — Berths can be secured in advance on payment of $25.00 per adult. Balances are payable three weeks before sailing.

CHILDREN'S FARES — Ten years and over, full fare; one year and under ten, half fare; under 1 year, $4.00.

INDEX

PUBLIC ROOMS	Odd Numbers Indicate Lowers
OUTSIDE ROOMS	Even Numbers Indicate Uppers
INSIDE ROOMS	☐ Indicate Wash Basin
	W. Indicate Wardrobe
BATHS AND LAVATORIES	☐ Indicate Folding Seat
	Indicate Settee

On C-deck, ample promenade deck space was combined with a children's playroom and large dolls' house, reading and writing room, dining saloon with dance floor, barber's shop and passenger staterooms. This dining saloon was previously the tourist third cabin dining saloon. (When this area was used as tourist third cabin, the space later occupied by the children's playroom and dolls' house had been used as accommodation for the chief tourist steward and the purser's office; the reading and writing room had also been much smaller, before it was enlarged at the expense of the dining saloon.)(Author's collection)

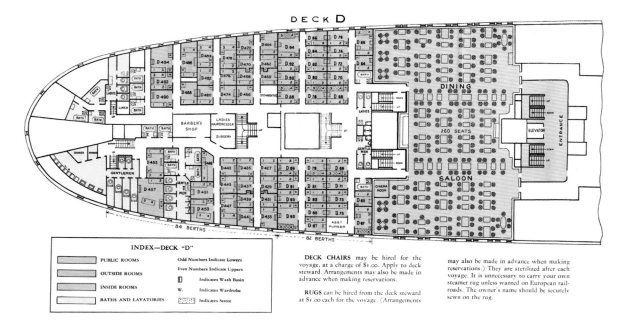

DECK D

D 454
D 492
D 490
D 488
D 486
D 482
D 480
D 484
D 478
D 476
D 474
D 472
D 470
D 468
D 466
D 464
D 462
D 460
D 94
D 92
D 90
D 88
D 86
D 84
D 82
D 80
D 78
D 76
D 74
D 72
D 70
D 68
D 66
D 64

BATH
LADIES
LINEN
BATH
BATH
BATH
BATH
SHOWER
GENTLEMEN

BARBER'S SHOP
LADIES HAIRDRESSER
SURGERY

STEWARDS

LADIES

GENTLEMEN

DINING

260 SEATS

SALOON

ELEVATOR

ENTRANCE

D 455
D 445
D 457
D 451
D 453
GENTLEMEN

D 443
D 445
D 447
D 435
D 437
D 439
D 441
D 427
D 429
D 431
D 433
D 89
D 91
D 93
D 95
D 79
D 81
D 83
D 85
D 87
D 69
D 71
D 73
D 75
D 77
D 67
D 65

CINEMA ROOM
BATH

ASST PURSER

84 BERTHS
82 BERTHS

INDEX—DECK "D"

PUBLIC ROOMS	Odd Numbers Indicate Lowers
OUTSIDE ROOMS	Even Numbers Indicate Uppers
INSIDE ROOMS	☐ Indicates Wash Basin
	W. Indicates Wardrobe
BATHS AND LAVATORIES	Indicates Settee

DECK CHAIRS may be hired for the voyage, at a charge of $1.00. Apply to deck steward. Arrangements may also be made in advance when making reservations.

RUGS can be hired from the deck steward at $1.00 each for the voyage. (Arrangements

may also be made in advance when making reservations.) They are sterilized after each voyage. It is unnecessary to carry your own steamer rug unless wanted on European railroads. The owner's name should be securely sewn on the rug.

On D-deck, accommodation included many staterooms at the stern and the former second-class dining saloon: 'Here you pick up your napkin and settle down for a real meal – plentiful and well cooked. After hours in the sun and wind, how welcome is the profusion of the menu! The food is well served, too, by attentive waiters.' (Author's collection)

DECK E

152 BERTHS   124 BERTHS   141 BERTHS

SERVICE—*Majestic* service is modern, unobtrusive and gracious. Bedroom and bath stewards cater to your early morning needs . . . Dining-room stewards are unfailingly courteous . . . deck stewards strive to satisfy all your wants. No matter where you roam on this great ship, there are always groups of well-trained servants anxious to serve and assist you.

INDEX

OUTSIDE ROOMS	Odd Numbers Indicate Lowers
INSIDE ROOMS	Even Numbers Indicate Uppers
	☐ Indicate Wash Basin
BATHS AND LAVATORIES	W. Indicate Wardrobe
	Indicate Settee

ADDRESSES—Travelers are advised to leave their addresses with the company when booking passage; with the ship's purser when landing, and with their friends and their bankers when traveling. Address cards are provided at our ticket offices and on our steamers.

On E-deck, accommodation consisted of many passenger staterooms (and there were similar staterooms on F-deck beneath). (Author's collection)

Cunard White Star issued a brochure for eastbound travellers advertising the tourist-class passenger accommodation on the ships in their combined fleet: 'Tourist class passengers in Cunard White Star ships today may enjoy many luxuries usually reserved for first class passengers, such as staterooms with private bath in the *Berengaria*, *Carinthia*, *Franconia*, *Majestic* and *Olympic*, use of the swimming pools in the *Aquitania*, *Berengaria*, *Britannic*, *Carinthia*, *Franconia* and *Georgic*, talking pictures [motion pictures or 'talkies'] etc.' The brochure was printed 17 April 1935, after *Olympic* had completed her final eastbound crossing; *Majestic*'s final crossing was less than a year away. (Author's collection)

MAJESTIC TOURIST CLASS

TOURIST CLASS accommodations in the Majestic are splendidly uncrowded. They live up to the glorious promise of space and freedom vividly suggested by this famous liner as it blocks the horizon with its sheer bigness and majesty. Staterooms in the Tourist Class of the Majestic are spacious . . . airy . . . cheerful. In some of the rooms real beds and running hot and cold water are available. Yet, because no one who is taking a transatlantic trip expects to remain cooped up inside, Cunard White Star have allotted an unusually generous deck area for Tourist Class use in the Majestic. There is plenty of room for the playing of exciting deck sports, or for exhilarating promenades over the vast decks, all the while you are drinking in a sense of power that only the Majestic can give.

The special Tourist Class dance floor is one of the ship's most attractive features. And it is especially popular with the younger set who quickly find that its fine parquet floor is smooth enough to satisfy the most ardent dancer and spacious enough to save wear and tear from the toes of fellow terpsichoreans. The handsome Tourist Class cocktail bar, a new feature of the Majestic, is much appreciated by passengers for that pre-dinner aperitif, after-dinner liqueur, or occasional tete-a-tete over a glass of cool, tinkling cheer.

An excellently equipped gymnasium, complete with the newest electrical gadgets, including an electric horse and camel, will tone up your muscles and keep you in fine physical trim. Pre-release talking pictures are shown in the Tourist Class dining room. This room at other times offers an unusually attractive setting for the superb culinary efforts of the Majestic's chefs.

Probably not the least of the worries of a family traveling Tourist Class is the care of the children. Yet on the Majestic this need not trouble you at all, for one of its chief attractions is a special children's play room, properly outfitted with playthings and decorated in glad Toyland style.

White Star advertised 'weekend cruises' from $50 and above when *Olympic* and *Majestic* undertook weekend cruises to Halifax in summer 1931. All passengers were accommodated as first class. (Günter Bäbler collection)

A large group of passengers pose beside the dance floor in tourist class during a July 1935 crossing (see page 112). (Mike Poirier collection)

... and others take the sea air. Sadly, the summer of 1935 marked *Majestic*'s last in service. Less than a year later, she was withdrawn from service. (Mike Poirier collection)

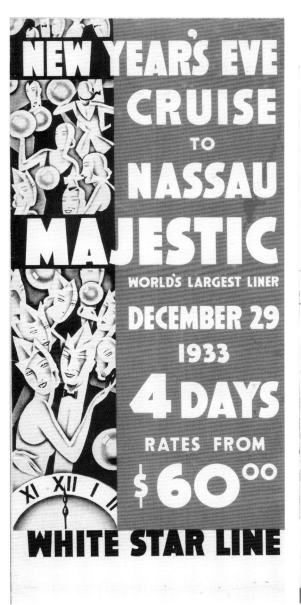

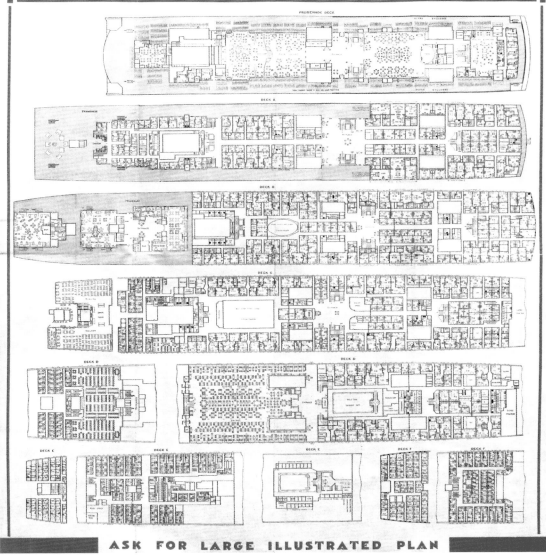

White Star advertised *Majestic*'s New Year's Cruise for 1934: 'Don't do the ordinary thing this New Year's Eve – dinner and the theatre and dancing on a floor so crowded that your feet can't find a spot. We give you the *Majestic* and everything she has to offer for four days ...' The brochure was issued on 15 November 1933 at New York. (Two years later, the New Year's Cruise for 1936 was advertised for five days at $60, making it even cheaper because there was an extra day for the same price.) (Author's collection)

Majestic was effectively a one-class ship again for her New Year's Cruise for 1934. Passengers had the run of the first- and tourist-class accommodation. These accommodation plans show the extent of the public rooms and facilities available. (Author's collection)

Inside a giant WHITE STAR LINER

SALE CATALOGUE

"MAJESTIC"

FURNISHINGS · PANELLING
APPOINTMENTS · FITTINGS

TWW

Far left: In this stylish illustration, White Star wanted to encourage prospective passengers up the gangway. (Author's collection)

The front cover of the auction catalogue included an imposing illustration of *Majestic*. The attached conditions included: 'Baths, Basins and all articles connected to supply piping are sold exclusive of supply piping unless otherwise stated'; 'Delivery, as and where lying on ship, unless otherwise arranged'; Terms were 'nett cash. Payment must be made before the articles leave the ship, and deposits are respectfully requested at the time of purchase'; and 'Visitors are requested not to smoke whilst on the ship'. (Author's collection)

HMS *Caledonia* (as depicted in Volume 2 of *The Caledonia Journal*, issued December 1938.) (Author's collection)

Below: The reverse of a postcard advertising the auction of *Majestic*'s fittings at Southampton. (Mike Poirier collection)

POST CARD.

CORRESPONDENCE.

FOR THE ADDRESS ONLY.

POSTAGE.

The "MAJESTIC'S" MAGNIFICENT PANELLINGS & FITTINGS NOW ON SALE NEW DOCK, SOUTHAMPTON

Admission to Ship by Catalogue only, price 1/3 each, from Ship or—

THOS W. WARD LTD. ALBION WORKS SHEFFIELD

R.M.S. "MAJESTIC."
Ladies' & Gentlemen's Hairdressing Saloon (D Deck)

APPOINTMENT CARD.

Passengers are respectfully requested to keep their appointed time within Five Minutes, otherwise the appointment will be cancelled.

Date	Time	Description

An appointment card for the hairdressing saloon on board. It appears they did business while people were looking over the ship prior to the auction. (Author's collection)

CALEDONIA

HMS *CALEDONIA*

In 1936, Britain's existing naval training facilities were undergoing a considerable expansion. The Admiralty considered three options for *Majestic*: buying the ship outright, hiring her with an option to purchase, or simply hiring her: 'If we must get the *Majestic* [from Thomas Ward's] the best course will be to purchase her outright on the understanding that the firm will buy her back when the Admiralty have finished, at a figure to be agreed.' One advantage of purchasing passenger liners was that at the end of their service as shore-based training facilities they would still have a good value as scrap, whereas temporary constructions would not. Unfortunately for them, they had to pay £140,000 (significantly higher than her sale price only a few months earlier).

The Admiralty chose to use Messrs. J.I. Thornycroft & Co. to complete the conversion work 'in preference' to Harland & Wolff and 'without further negotiation' with the Belfast shipbuilder. The basis for their decision was that Thornycroft 'had stated they would be satisfied with a profit of 7½ per cent', whereas Harland & Wolff 'had spoken of 10 per cent'. Their rate might have been negotiated downwards but the Admiralty took it as 'evidence that Messrs. Thornycroft would do the work on better terms'. They were concerned that, although both firms had capable repair establishments at Southampton, Thornycroft also had an adjacent shipbuilding yard and 'were better equipped to meet the unforeseen demands which were likely to arise …'

They thought Thornycroft were 'more likely to complete the work on time, and emphasized the serious expense resulting from a delay on a contract … made on a cost plus profit basis'. On 27 August 1936, the naval authorities confirmed their instructions: 'the work is to be taken in hand as early as possible … to enable the vessel to be delivered to Rosyth by you by the end of February 1937 …' It was 'essential that the amount of work performed should be strictly limited to that which is necessary to adapt the ship for her new service'. Admiralty representatives would be visiting frequently to monitor progress. 'You are required to take full responsibility and custody of the vessel from midnight on the 31st August …' Work began on 2 September 1936. *Majestic*'s new name, *Caledonia*, was being used by 4 December 1936.

John Havers recalled seeing her funnels and masts shortened. He saw her on 10 December 1936 in the graving dock at Southampton and ten days later saw her leave the dock to berth with her port side to the quay. The conversion took longer than original expectations. On 8 April 1937, he was up early and saw *Caledonia* sail from Southampton for the last time: 'She passed by with blinding clouds of smoke belching from her shortened funnels. She had a sort of fighting top with her name in red and also in gold letters on the aft end of the boat deck. Funnels were dark yellow. She had nets visible and semaphores.'[1]

Majestic looks the worse for wear in this photograph taken on 4 December 1936, when she entered dry dock at Southampton. The majority of lifeboats have been removed, as well as various deck fittings. The tops of all three funnels have been cut down and reduced in height (the first funnel was cut down first), as have the fore and aft masts. This preparatory work was necessary so that she would be able to pass under the bridge when she steamed through the Firth of Forth at Rosyth, Scotland. The *Liverpool Journal of Commerce* listed her as one of a number of 'vessels in dry dock' on Saturday, 5 December 1936: '*Caledonia* (HMS) (ex *Majestic*)'. (*Süddeutsche Zeitung* Photo/Alamy Stock Photo)

Majestic cut an imposing profile docked at Southampton. Looking up from the dockside, her funnels were barely visible. The name has still not been changed on her bow. (*Süddeutsche Zeitung* Photo/Alamy Stock Photo)

The view from *Majestic*'s bow, docked at Southampton. (Richard Sloan collection)

The construction of a boxing ring in what was originally the first-class lounge. On 1 December 1936, the *Yorkshire Evening Post* quoted Svend Larsen, managing director of Niels Larsen & Son Ltd (Leeds), saying that his company had secured a contract for 'one of the biggest orders our firm has ever had for gymnastic apparatus'. He explained: 'There will be 36 climbing ropes, 63 wall bars, 16 balancing forms, and eight sets of counterbalanced gymnastic beams, as well as a large boxing ring. The work is to be finished in eight weeks. It is possible that some of our work people from Leeds will have to work aboard the *Majestic* while the liner is at sea on her voyage to Rosyth ...' (Richard Sloan collection)

Few, if any, of the ship's company in H.M.S. ' Caledonia' would recognise in this one of their class rooms of to-day ! Actually, our picture was obtained whilst we were converting the vessel from an Atlantic liner to an important unit of His Majesty's Navy, and when it is remembered that she is still the third largest vessel afloat those who have served in her can imagine the magnitude of our task—and see how well we succeeded ! But this is not our only association with the Senior Service. Many an old tar could tell of Thornycroft boats long in commission when they were boys, and of famous vessels from our yard which have since engraved their names in History. To-day, we are engaged in producing a variety of craft—T.B.D.'s, sloops, motor torpedo boats, and smaller types—further to uphold the prestige and efficiency of the greatest navy in the world.

*

JOHN I. THORNYCROFT & CO., LIMITED, WOOLSTON WORKS, SOUTHAMPTON

Clockwise from above: This photograph in a Thornycroft advertisement shows what was formerly passenger accommodation on one of the ship's lower decks. The non-structural bulkheads and stateroom fittings all had to be removed, which was a lengthy and complicated task. (Jim Duckworth collection)

When the conversion was completed, the original first-class dining saloon retained much of its original grandeur. However, the lengthy rows of tables for the boys' mess were much less comfortable than the original separate tables for first-class passengers. (Jim Duckworth collection)

One of the compartments on F-deck sits largely empty, prior to conversion to sleeping accommodation. The ship's frames and the curve of the hull are visible to the right. The line of pillars formed part of the ship's hull and were an important component of the structure, providing strength and supporting the decks. (Jim Duckworth collection)

H.M.S. 'CALEDONIA'

once the "Majestic" and the world's biggest ship, leaving Southampton for Rosyth after conversion as a naval training ship by John I. Thornycroft & Co., Limited. This vessel is still the third largest in size afloat being surpassed only by "Queen Mary" and the "Normandie," and the reconstruction was no mean undertaking.

✳

JOHN I. **THORNYCROFT** AND CO., LIMITED

Shipbuilders & Engineers

WOOLSTON WORKS, SOUTHAMPTON

Caledonia leaves Southampton on 8 April 1937, with thick smoke rising from her shortened funnels. Thornycroft were proud of their work and were keen to emphasise that she was still ranked the third largest ship in the world. (Jim Duckworth collection)

Aquitania passed the pier around the same time, bound for the graving dock. The *New York Times* recalled that *Majestic* had 'for more than a dozen years … reigned supreme' and opined: 'she probably will never again pit her 56,600 tons against an angry sea'. One observer looked back on all of the work needed to transform her, and her journey to Rosyth:

First of all, the general layout was planned; that is to say hospital wards, classrooms, sleeping spaces, bathrooms and wash places were mapped out, and a start was made on the work of stripping out all unwanted fittings. Those who only know the ship as she is today would get a considerable shock if they could see what they now know to be orderly classrooms, the spic and span hospital or large shower baths, littered with electric wires and plumbers' fittings, with broken decks and scarred paint. Indeed, it was difficult to believe that order would ever come out of the chaos which greeted you on all sides, but with over 2,000 men working from 7 o'clock in the morning until 8 o'clock at night, every day of the week, the task was accomplished in eight months.

Difficulties and handicaps of all descriptions had to be overcome; having planned a bank of classrooms it would be discovered when the space was cleared, that solid steel structures blocked the way and could not be removed. Where bathrooms or washplaces had been planned, difficulty arose over getting the water supply to that place or the drainage away from it. Trade in the South of England was flourishing at that time and the services of draughtsmen and joiners were practically impossible to obtain, with the result that work got out of step with the planning. But despite these difficulties, the ship left Southampton under her own steam on 8 April 1937, under the command of Captain J.W. Binks, who had commanded such fine ships as the *Olympic*. The trip up the North Sea was without incident and the weather was fine for the whole journey. After the hustle and bustle of the previous six months everything appeared remarkably silent. On arrival in the Firth of Forth, on Saturday 10 April, the ship was anchored below Inchkeith and waited until the state of the tide was suitable for her to proceed up the estuary, pass under the Forth Bridge and be locked in the basin. For this operation she was assisted by seven tugs from Hull and Grangemouth. This last part of the proceedings required skill and judgement on the part of the officers responsible. With her great length and beam it was a delicate operation, only possible at the most favourable state of the tide. All went well, however, and the ship finally secured alongside her new permanent berth and the work of connecting up all the necessary services from the shore went ahead without delay.

As she is now, the ship has accommodation for 100 Officers, 180 Chief and Petty Officers, a Ship's Company of 300, 1,500 Boys and 500 Artificer Apprentices. The ship is entirely self-contained as far as the domestic services are concerned, i.e., heat, light, power and hot water are all generated on board and fresh water is led into the ship direct from the shore supply.

The food for the whole ship's company and for the boys is cooked in one central galley with all store rooms, preparing rooms, issuing rooms and offices in the immediate vicinity. The efficiency of the department, which is always considered one of the most important in the Navy, is greatly increased by this arrangement. Many might pause and consider for a moment the amount of work and organisation required in order to produce hot and appetising meals for 2,500 people exactly to time. On either side of this galley are the main dining halls for the boys and the apprentices. On the fore side, the old first class dining saloon now seats 1,200 boys at one time, at tables

and stools of the same pattern as any broadside mess of a man-of-war, but they may still gaze upwards at the country scene, painted on the domed ceiling, which no doubt many transatlantic passengers have admired on the after side, the old second class dining saloon accommodates 500 Artificer Apprentices in the same way.

The sick quarters, containing eight wards, are fully equipped to deal with cases of injury and disease, including infectious cases.

There are a modern X-ray department, an operating theatre fitted with the latest equipment and anaesthetic apparatus, a laboratory, and a massage and electrical treatment centre.

The staff of four Medical Officers includes a Surgical Specialist …

The ship's public rooms changed substantially:

What was the first class lounge has been converted into a small but very popular gymnasium, where church services are held on Sundays and where concerts, lectures and, it is hoped, cinema shows will be given.

The first class palm court serves as a general recreation room with a well-stocked canteen at one end, together with ping-pong tables, a wireless receiver and pictures of general interest. The swimming bath is still used as such, and those boys who can swim pass their swimming test in a duck suit, and those who cannot swim at all are given instruction in this necessary art. The other services in the ship which have to receive consideration are, to mention a few, the clothing issue room where every new recruit receives his first suit of navy blue and from whence replenishments are made as required; the tailor's shop where a staff works hard at fitting new kits and dealing with repairs; a boot repairer's shop which is kept continuously busy; the barber's shop; and the laundry and drying rooms where each boy learns to do his own washing. For recreation there are rugby, soccer, cricket and hockey pitches, the number of which will be doubled in the near future. Fixtures are obtained in all these games with local schools and clubs with a similar standard of play. A .22 rifle range is a popular place to spend an hour or two and there are competitions and prizes to be won by the best shots.

Costs had spiralled far beyond initial estimates. The Treasury became alarmed and the Admiralty delayed telling them until practically all the work had been done and the money spent. (The cost was not revealed until July 1938, immediately prior to a Parliamentary Public Accounts Committee Report that contained comments 'relating to the very large expenditure involved in the conversion of the SS *Majestic* into a Boy's Training Establishment'.) When the Treasury had sanctioned the work in October 1936, they had been led to believe that the conversion would cost about £150,000; in the event this soared to £472,000, with £326,000 spent in 1936–37 and the remainder in 1937–38. Much of the cost related to unexpected work that needed to be done on the old liner, and the officials emphasised that there were always problems in estimating the work that needed to be done until everything was already in hand:

> During the progress of the work the pipe systems opened up so badly that extensive renewals of innumerable parts were necessary. A similar state of decay was found throughout on other machinery equipment and such expensive items as the complete renewal of tubes in the auxiliary condensers, cylinders and barrels for pumps and large repairs of bunkers and boilers were necessary. The bulk of the expenditure on machinery was in respect of equipment which is now in daily use under auxiliary steam.

The additional expenses included all manner of things, from fumigating 'the ship at Southampton on account of vermin'; to fitting additional apartments on C-deck 'for sisters and maids in connection with the hospital arrangements'; and general restoration work: 'the ship's hull and fittings on opening up were found to be in a more unsatisfactory state

Caledonia in the Firth of Forth on 10 April 1937 ... (Author's collection)

... and continues on to her final destination. (Author's collection)

than expected and substantial unanticipated expense arose in repairing, modifying, renovating, painting, etc. to bring the vessel up to the required standard'. The work was 'considered to have been necessary for the purpose of producing an efficient and hygienic training ship in a short space of time … the expenditure incurred was unavoidable'. (The accounting officer of the navy noted that *Caledonia* was ready long before an establishment ashore could have been completed and 'the Admiralty are now hopeful that it will be possible to use the ship for at least ten years to come' in March 1938.)

Despite all the budgetary concerns, she was officially commissioned on 23 April 1937. The first boys came on board in May 1937 and the number of boys 'under instruction' rose steadily:

HMS *Caledonia*	May 1937	12 June 1937	10 July 1937	7 August 1937	4 September 1937	2 October 1937	1 April 1938
Boys	35	163	309	388	619	833	1,643

In this rare view of *Caledonia* docked at Rosyth, it is easy to imagine how the *Majestic* may have looked in her prime, speeding across the dark Atlantic leaving very little wake. Unfortunately, the crane spoils the *Caledonia*'s profile somewhat. (Imperial War Museum, HU75155)

In 1937, cadets of the ship's company march past King George VI, accompanied by Queen Elizabeth and Princess Elizabeth (later Queen Elizabeth II), who receives the salute. (Imperial War Museum, HU75151)

In July 1937, 'a contingent of boys lined the streets of Edinburgh' and were 'marched past their Majesties the King and Queen at the Palace of Holyroodhouse'. Lieutenant J. Wilson noted the daily routine that applied when he was in training during 1938 and 1939:

Time	Activity
5 a.m.	Call the Hands.
5–6 a.m.	Lash up and stow hammocks, wash, dress, and a snack of cocoa and a ship's biscuit.
6–7 a.m.	Scrub decks (barefoot). Holy stone (on hands and knees). Squee-gee dry. Polish all brass.
7–8 a.m.	Breakfast. Clean into dress of the day.
8 a.m.–12 p.m.	Divisions, prayers and colours. This was followed by three sessions of instruction, school, seamanship, gunnery, etc. 'Standeasy' was within this period and consisted of a cup of tea and a doughnut.
12–1 p.m.	Hands to dinner, usually a three-course meal of soup, main course, and a sweet.

1-4 p.m.	Games and sport on the playing fields of Rosyth. Each boy was issued with a pair of white shorts and a white jersey for the English or a blue one for the Scottish. Daily orders listed the type of game, who was in which team and which strip to be worn. Whether one knew the laws of a particular game or not, one soon learnt.
4-4.30 p.m.	Tea. Bread with jam, marmalade or syrup. Change into night clothing, which included a pair of comfortable, brown canvas shoes with leather toe-caps.
4.30-7 p.m.	Evening quarters and evening instruction.
7-9 p.m.	Supper followed by recreation time. During this time, boys had to take a shower and change into pyjamas for 'short arm' inspection before turning in.
9 p.m.	Lightsout [*sic*] and pipedown.

One of the apprentices (or 'apps') wrote an article for *The Caledonia Magazine* describing his life on board in 1937. He hoped to 'settle the minds of many other boys who do not know what career to adopt':

Our quarters are aft, and consist of a regulating office, dining hall, four sleeping decks, four bathrooms, and two recreation rooms. The regulating office is the control room where all disciplinary matters are dealt with. On the sleeping decks are metal lockers big enough to hold an Apprentices' kit, and overhead are steel rails from which the hammocks are 'slung' at night. The bathrooms are small, but after a bit of a 'rough house', enjoyed by all, we may, given reasonable luck, wash successfully. The mess-rooms and recreation spaces are kept clean by pensioners. The number of Apprentices on one 'mess table' is usually sixteen, and arrangements are often made to 'club together' to buy extras and trifles. In the recreation rooms are ping pong tables, darts, table games, daily papers and periodicals. In the senior recreation rooms there are sofas, but juniors wait until they pass the age of eighteen before they can sit in comfort!!! The quarters are always clean, and anyone found dirtying them 'catches it hot'.

Apprentices are divided into four divisions 'Anson' – 'Rodney' – 'Grenville' and 'Hawke', the latter are the new Special Entry and are all over eighteen and have been Apprentices for $2^{1}/_{2}$ years with outside firms, therefore enjoying privileges as seniors.

After joining, an Apprentice does a fourteen days Disciplinary Course during which time are taught Seamanship, Squad and Rifle Drill, before going to the workshops where he is issued with a set of tools. After three months, we do our first future 'test job' – a plate and prism which is a test of chipping and accurate fitting. Our future trade depends upon the result of this job, and we become either boilermakers, enginesmiths, coppersmiths, or fitters and turners. During the first two years we do a course of fitting on the benches from which we go on, when proficient, to machines and lathes. Later, we practise 'trueing up' flanges, re-seating valves, refitting small engines or pumps, and various jobs to give us an idea of what is expected of an Artificer in workshops afloat …

Recreation is an important part of our training, but there is not enough of it. We go to the gym two hours a week to be strengthened and hardened. Once weekly, in addition to Saturday afternoon, we play Hockey, Soccer and Rugby in the winter, Cricket, Tennis and Swimming in the summer – we also have Sailing, Boat pulling, Rifle Shooting and cross Country runs. The Swimming bath aboard, a great asset during the winter months, is also available for our pleasure on certain evenings during the week. Each recreation afternoon, Football matches, competitive games, and races take place between us and the Seamen Boys or alternatively with other schools in the vicinity. Every Apprentice takes part in some form of sport. The Divisional spirit in 'Anson' and 'Rodney' is very strong, while in the 'Grenville' the newcomers, it is most promising. The ship's Rugger team, which is most popular, has a large proportion of Apprentices in it, but as regards Soccer our representatives are not so common, and hope to be in the majority in the near future. Our Cross Country team and Cutters crews go out every Saturday for practice. The gymnasium is always available during our leisure hours, and Boxing, Concert Parties and Lectures covering subjects which interest the majority of Apprentices prove a great attraction.

'The life of an apprentice on board *Caledonia* is really good, although as is common in all spheres of life, at times it seems monotonous and tiresome,' he concluded: 'There are far more incidents to laugh over, than cry over, when the day is finished. I hope that if anyone, after reading this article "joins up", they will not blame me if they do not like it here. If they are average, decent and honest lads, they are almost sure to enjoy it.' (On the other hand, Tom Robson thought 'discipline was very strict'. He recalled several occasions when boys deserted and were later arrested.)

This photograph, from Rev. J.N.C. Holland's collection, shows a group of the ship's officers on board at Rosyth. Rev. Holland, the chaplain of the Boys' Training Establishment, is standing second left in the second row. (Imperial War Museum, HU75152)

Caledonia cuts an impressive profile behind the ship's company and a band of the Royal Marines, who are visible in the foreground. (Imperial War Museum, HU75150)

Boys from the Grenville Division. 'To the "Grenvilles" has fallen the distinction of being the first apprentices to join the Mechanical Training Establishment of the North ...' (Jim Duckworth collection)

The boys' work included maintenance and all ships needed plenty of paint to keep them looking good: 'The B-deck painting party.' (Jim Duckworth collection)

Caledonia's pool looked much the same as it had when first-class passengers used it. The boys certainly made use of it. (Jim Duckworth collection)

The Foretop Division pose for a group photograph off *Caledonia*'s aft port quarter. (Jim Duckworth collection)

In December 1937 proposals were being drawn up about what to do with the ship in the event of war. *Caledonia* was berthed alongside the West Wall of the Main Basin in Rosyth's Naval Dockyard, the only suitable berth for her where she could function as a training ship. If hostilities broke out, this would be the most important berth in the dockyard for refitting ships, and her presence rendered it impossible to use the capstans there (which were necessary for docking all heavy ships, especially in bad weather). And whatever would happen if the ship caught fire?

Danger of Fire – A serious fire in *Caledonia* would almost certainly cause damage to either the structure or electric supply to the 250-ton crane, putting it out of action. The danger would also exist of fires being started in other parts of the Dockyard or in other ships through burning material falling at a distance away from *Caledonia*, particularly in a high wind …

Nor could the necessary water level be guaranteed with frequent visits to the basin by other vessels, regardless of the tide. During the First World War, both main dock pumps had been running for twenty-four hours to keep the basin topped up but, even so, the water level shrank by 6in since it was in constant use by many ships.

Another problem concerned the question of the 2,000 boys on board. Clearly they could not remain on board the ship, in an area 'which might be the target for an air attack'. They would need to be evacuated on the outbreak of war. One assumption that the ship herself would remain in the dockyard was awkward, since she was a great target for enemy air attack: 'A direct hit from an explosive or incendiary bomb would be particularly disastrous, as unlike a warship, the majority of the interior bulkheads are of wood.' Rear Admiral Thomson recommended that the *Caledonia* should be removed from the basin and anchored in the river, clear of the Fleet Anchorage. This would require a tow for the ship since her engines were 'not being kept in a state of repair'. Early in 1938 it was confirmed that she would be removed in the event of war breaking out. Meanwhile, the Board of Trade had to see about closing their file on the ship. On 8 March 1939 the Board wrote: 'This vessel, which was refitted to be a training ship by the Admiralty, is not ever likely to return to service as a passenger ship.'[2]

The Admiralty identified that 'the vulnerability of this huge ship had led to the conclusion that she was useless to us as a training establishment in time of war'. Naturally, they acted accordingly when war broke out. At the start of September 1939, the authorities arranged for the boys and staff to transfer to HMS *St George*, on the Isle of Man. (The establishment became the Training Establishment for Continuous Service Seaman Boys.) Walter J. Braddock recalled *Caledonia*'s final days and Prime Minister Neville Chamberlain's announcement that the United Kingdom was now at war with Germany:

Saturday 2nd September was a tense day and shore leave was cancelled because no answer had been received to the ultimatum to Germany and there was apprehension that the Germans might try a surprise air or sea attack without war being declared. We worked ship as usual and were told to get all our kit together …

Sunday 3rd September was Sunday routine as usual, clean shop, breakfast, clean into number ones, divisions at 0900 hours followed by church. We knew there was going to be an announcement at 1100 hours over the radio so divisions and church were completed in rather less time than usual and we went to our mess decks and gathered near the tannoy speakers to hear the fateful broadcast by Mr. Chamberlain.

S.S. " LEVIATHAN " AND H.M.S. " CALEDONIA."

Leviathan (left) arrives for scrapping in 1938. Although *Majestic* was the first of the three sisters to be withdrawn permanently from passenger service, by 1939 she was the only one that had not been scrapped. In March 1939, the Board of Trade concluded that she would never return to passenger service; she had served almost two years as *Caledonia* (right). One of the boys, R.D. Horn, wrote a poem to mark the occasion:

Our Sister's Fate

When spring was breaking o'er our ship,
Leviathan made a last, long trip.
Here she will terminate her days –
The final parting of their ways.

But such is fate.

Side by side the pair were laid –
The Teutons built them and, when made,
They idled through war's four long years,
While o'er the world ran wet, salt tears.

But such is fate.

When strife at last came to an end,
Their fortunes took a diff'rent trend.
The *Vaterland* went o'er the sea;
The other came to this country.

But such is fate.

Together then they ploughed the foam,
Though each could boat a diff'rent home.
Majestic – largest ship afloat;
Leviathan – the New World's boat.

But such is fate.

Our craft gave place to larger ships,
To others now upon the slips;
To Scotia's shore one ploughed her way
To live, as 'Cal', another day.

But such is fate.

When spring was breaking o'er our ship,
Our sister made a last, long trip.
Here she will terminate her days –
The final parting of their ways.

R.D. Horn, Grenville [Division]. (Jim Duckworth collection)

There was no cheering, but a lot of serious faces and a general air of relief that, at last, the uncertainty was over, few comments 'well that's that' and 'now we know' seemed to sum it up. I think we all wondered what was going to happen but no one was going to show that they were afraid. We didn't have much time for contemplation, for within a few minutes, the air raid sirens sounded and we went into our, long practised, air raid drill, rapidly left the ship, fell in by divisions on the jetty and doubled off into the dockyard to our designated shelters in the underground passages around the dry-docks. It seems it was a false alarm or an exercise for after half-an-hour the 'all clear' sounded and we trooped back onto the ship. Instructions came over the tannoy that we clean into number threes and overalls, go to dinner, and all-hand fall-in for work would be at 1330 hours. Dinner was the last cooked meal on the ship.

At 1315 hours we were detailed off into working parties to lift all moveable stores and kit out of the ship, onto the jetty, and into a number of dockyard lorries which then transported their loads across the dockyard to the railway sidings where, unknown to us, some days previously, three long trains of carriages and wagons had been drawn up. Into these went everything moveable … By 1830 hours, everything was loaded into the trains, there was a roll call muster by classes, then we entrained and away we went.

The last we saw of the ship was the view of her against the sunset sky as we went over the Forth Bridge heading south …

While the Admiralty had come up with a plan to refit her as a transport, it would never come to fruition.[3] On 30 September 1939, *The Scotsman* reported 'an outbreak of fire occurred on HMS *Caledonia* yesterday. The ship was seen to be on fire about four o'clock yesterday morning. Flames came from all parts of the *Caledonia*, and the fire continued for some hours. It was subdued during the afternoon…' The *Dundee Courier and Advertiser* said that 'the outbreak was first discovered between 3 and 4 a.m.' and it was 'impracticable to fight the fire with adequate resources'. The smoke 'could be seen for several miles': 'The ship was badly damaged amidships and the hull severely scarred. It is understood there was no one aboard when the fire started …' The *Northern Whig and Belfast Post* said 'a red glow was seen below the deck and a pall of smoke hung over the ship'. The *Daily Record and Mail* reported 'since the outbreak of war, only six watchmen have been stationed on the *Caledonia*': 'at dusk dense clouds of smoke were still coming from the vessel'. The *Dundee Evening Telegraph* explained 'it is understood that the outbreak may have been caused by a faulty electric circuit. The fire was so fierce that it was impossible to get near the ship to attempt to quell the flames. Tons of burning fuel spread over the water for about 300 yards.'

The fire 'burnt her almost completely out, she is reduced to a hulk, and is now grounded on the Tancred Bank in the Firth of Forth', wrote an Admiralty official on 3 November 1939.

'Repairs sufficient to equip her for any war or peacetime purpose would be extremely expensive.' Thomas Ward's had been in contact 'asking to be allowed to make an offer' to buy her back. Plenty of discussion followed. By 27 February 1940, the Admiralty had:

> reached the conclusion that for the present it will be best not to sell the ship outright for breaking up, but merely to remove and dispose of the top hamper: if the vessel were sold for breaking up it would be necessary to raise her and remove her to a breaking up yard. In view of the frequent visits of enemy aircraft to the Forth there would be a risk of the vessel being sunk in the fairway if she were moved …

Thomas Ward's did not want to make an outright offer for the entire wreck but they could 'remove the top hamper and dispose of it'. The Treasury agreed in March 1940 and Thomas Ward's had completed the work by 8 July 1941: 'it is understood … that some 7,000 tons of scrap have been recovered'. There was 'an acute shortage of scrap' metal in the United Kingdom and the Ministry of Supply advocated the 'total demolition' of the remainder of the hull by handing her over to the British Iron & Steel Corporation (Salvage) Limited, which was a non-profit company formed 'for the purpose of recovering material from wrecks'. They estimated that there were 30–40,000 tons of scrap left to be recovered and the Corporation would employ Thomas Ward's 'to carry out the dismantling operations'. They would 'make the vessel watertight, partially raise her and gradually drag her into shallower water, removing material at each stage until the mean draught is reduced to about 15 feet (her present draught is about 20 feet forward and 30 feet aft'). A Treasury official agreed with the proposals, adding: 'It is amusing that the Admiralty have now been persuaded to undertake the full salvage on which we were keen from the start.'

Looking forward along the port bow on 3 May 1942, the corrosion on the lower part of the hull is visible, as are the 'plugged' portholes, after *Caledonia* had been raised. Much of the hull plating has already been cut away, although some of the quadruple riveting is visible. (Imperial War Museum, A9766)

Caledonia's remnants were a sorry sight. (Imperial War Museum, A25218)

Work progressed steadily. Divers had to seal 1,800 ports as well as hull openings 'before she could be pumped dry'. On the first attempt, the hull was 'raised from deep water in the Fifth of Forth'. On 11 September 1942, the *Linlithgowshire Gazette* reported on a case of theft. Robert Ritchie, one of the salvage workers, had taken property including shoes, socks, shirts, cups, saucers, plates and aluminium bowls: 'The articles had been submerged some years, and were valued about £9 before submersion, but they would not be of much value today.' The 'inside of the ship was in a filthy, slimy and oily condition … the articles which had been submerged for so long had been in contact with these things. The socks, shirts, etc … were to be used as cleaning cloths.' The salvage work was under the control of Captain Bonar, VC, who was in court and attested to Ritchie's 'good character … He asked his Lordship to take a lenient view of the matter.' Ironically, Bonar would have let Ritchie take the articles away, if he had asked for them (except the metal items). Ritchie was fined £10 with the option of sixty days' imprisonment.

Gradually the hull plating was removed, save for the fore-peak, which was preserved in order to make it easier to tow the hulk. On 26 October 1942, officials agreed that dredging work could be done to create a channel sufficient 'to bring the hulk of *Caledonia* to Inverkeithing'. They thought 'there are still 20–30,000 tons of scrap involved' and 'recovery of the whole amount' would be possible. All in all, the liner provided 40,000 tons of 'first-class steel' for the British war effort. In 1943, the Admiralty were able to report that they had recovered 'sufficient steel to build between twelve and twenty cruisers'. *Bismarck/Majestic/Caledonia*'s life came to an end.

APPENDICES

APPENDIX 1

BRITISH REGISTRY DETAILS OF *MAJESTIC*

Official No. of Ship: 146,555

Length, between perpendiculars: 915ft 6in

Breadth: 100ft 1½in

Depth from top of deck at sides amidships to bottom of keel: 64ft 4in

Particulars of Displacement: 84,150 tons. Ditto per inch immersion at same depth: 175½ tons

No. of sets of engines: Eight

No. of shafts: Four

Description of Engines: Rotary steam compound or independent direct

Name and Address of Makers: Blohm & Voss, Hamburg, 1913–14

Rotary engines, No. of cylinders in each set: Eight sets (four ahead, four astern)

Shp: 66,000 ahead, 36,000 astern

Speed of Ship: 23 knots

Fuel: 8,717 tons oil fuel

Consumption per day: 840 tons (per 100 knots: 148 tons)

Particulars of Tonnage:

Gross tonnage 56,551.08 tons, net tonnage: 26,369.57 tons

Under tonnage deck: 13,829.30 tons

Space or Spaces Between Decks: 7,719.87 tons; 5,741.40 tons; 5,445.94 tons; 5,296.84 tons

Forecastle: 420.30 tons

Bridge Space: 9,088.20 tons

Side houses: 52.38 tons

Deck houses: 7,132.96 tons

Dated April 27th 1922

Number of Shares: 64

Date and Hour of Registry: May 1st 1922. 2 p.m.

Date of Transaction: Bill of Sale dated April 26th 1922

Name, Residence and Occupation of Transferee: Oceanic Steam Navigation Company Limited, having its principal place of business at 30 James Street in the City of Liverpool. Registry of the Vessel transferred to the Port of Liverpool this 1st day of May 1922. Certificate not issued.

Registered (net) tonnage altered to 26,323.96 December 1st 1922

Registered (net) tonnage altered to 26,258.83 August 12th 1925

Gross tonnage altered to 56,620.53; registered (net) tonnage altered to 26249.48 February 28th 1928

Gross tonnage altered to 56,598.71; registered (net) tonnage altered to 24,333.08 September 8th 1933

Cunard White Star Limited Bill of Sale dated June 3rd 1936 (Thos. W. Ward Limited)

Thos. W. Ward Limited Bill of Sale dated September 1st 1936 (His Majesty represented by the Commissioners for executing the office of Lord High Admiral of the United Kingdom of Great Britain and Ireland)

Cancelled and registry closed 21 July 1937. Registry no longer required. Advice received from the Lords Commissioners of the Admiralty.

APPENDIX 2

MAJESTIC PARTICULARS OF INTEREST

As specified on RMS *Majestic* first-class accommodation plans, 10 October 1928

'Particulars of interest':

Length of vessel: 956ft

Breadth: 100ft

Depth below water: 38ft

Height of sun deck above water: 70ft

Height of funnels above water: 150ft

Horizon distance from sun deck: 10 miles

Length of promenade deck: 500ft

Distance around promenade deck: Nearly ¼ mile

Weight of vessel: 64,500 tons

Gross tonnage: 56,621 tons

Shp: 66,000

Largest steamer in the world.

Majestic lives up to her name as she arrives in New York. This stunning photograph was taken from a plane. (See page 100, showing a period colour postcard that was, itself, based on a famous photo of *Majestic* showing the plane.)(Daniel Klistorner collection)

APPENDIX 3

'SOME INTERESTING FEATURES'

Extracted from the early 1920s brochure: '*Majestic* – The World's Largest Ship' (New York: White Star Line):

Majestic is fitted with all the latest accessories to comfort for passengers in all classes. Both steam and electricity are employed in heating public rooms and staterooms. A novel system of ventilation automatically ensures a constant supply of ozonized fresh air of proper temperature in all parts of the ship. The air is just as fresh in an inside as in an outside stateroom. All parts of the ship are electric lighted, more than 15,000 bulbs being used. When the public rooms are fully lighted the *Majestic* presents a brilliant spectacle. A complete telephone system connects all parts of the ship with a 'central'.

An outstanding novelty is a large public card room for the use of both sexes, situated on the promenade deck aft, where the smoking room is found on most ships. It is intended primarily for bridge and other socially approved card games. For children there is a special playroom, and also a special dining room. Maids and Valets have their own dining saloon. For sports the ship is specially equipped with a gymnasium, having an athletic instructor in charge; a special sports deck, with a variety of equipment; large squash racket courts, and, of course, the great swimming bath. Other special features are a darkroom for photographers, a shop selling travellers' necessaries and novelties; a large barber shop, and hairdressing parlours for women; a tailor's shop for repairing and pressing cloth-ing for both sexes; a conservatory for preserving flowers, and kennels for pet dogs.

Each class on the *Majestic* has its own kitchens, pantries and culinary and serving staff. There are no less than eight kitchens on the ship, a separate one being provided in third class for Jewish passengers requiring kosher food. The crew of 1,000 also have their own galleys and cooks.

Second and third cabin accommodations are unusually fine. The spacious and handsomely decorated second cabin lounge, reading room and smoking room open off a large and handsome foyer. The second cabin dining saloon, seating 500, has direct communication by electric elevator with this foyer. Second class staterooms cause delighted comment, and there are extensive promenade decks for this class. Third class also has its lounge, smoking room and dining saloon, all handsomely fitted, and many airy, well lighted two-, three- and four-berth staterooms.

The bedroom, dining room and kitchen equipment of the *Majestic* in the aggregate weighs many tons. There are 17 tons of blankets alone. Mattresses total 3,000, pillows 2,700 and bolsters 1,500. There are 75 tons of dishes, cooking utensils and bedroom crockery, and more than three tons of silverware and cutlery. No less than 190,000 pieces of linen are required, with 77,000 towels, 13,000 pillow cases, 8,000 bedspreads, 11,000 sheets, 10,500 blankets and 600 quilts … The cups side by side would fill a rack a mile long.

APPENDIX 4

MAJESTIC & BERENGARIA PROFITS AND LOSSES

In December 1938, Cunard White Star's accountants' department in Liverpool produced detailed summaries of the 'financial results of operating' *Berengaria* and *Majestic* over their careers for Cunard, White Star and Cunard White Star. They looked at the revenues (receipts) and expenses (disbursements) to determine the gross profit or loss, then the organisation expenses (such as advertising costs and repairs) that were deducted to determine the net profit or loss. They looked at the totals rather than the average per voyage.[1] On a headline basis, *Majestic* earned more net profit in total from 1922 to 1936 than *Berengaria* did over a longer period from 1921 to 1938, but *Berengaria* did better during 1923 to 1935 (the complete years each ship was in service).

However, their analysis of each ship's profit relative to its cost was striking. They took the total net profit and then subtracted a charge for depreciation, which they took as the cost of each ship (the purchase price minus the amount received from selling each ship). *Berengaria* had cost £734,321 (allowing for her £500,000 purchase price, plus money Cunard spent refitting her and minus the sale price), whereas *Majestic* had cost £1,467,773 (the 'prime cost' of £1,581,108, presumably including refits, minus the '£113,335 net realised on sale'). As a result, *Berengaria* had made a total profit of £1,414,878 'available towards dividends' against *Majestic*'s £795,180: *Berengaria*'s average per year worked out to 10.7 per cent of the cost of the ship, whereas *Majestic*'s worked out to 3.9 per cent. This reflected the commercial reality that each ship had a similar earning power and yet Cunard had paid significantly less for *Berengaria* compared to White Star's cost for *Majestic*. Overall, *Berengaria* generated a profit available for dividends of 192 per cent of her purchase price, whereas *Majestic* generated 54 per cent.

BERENGARIA

Year	Receipts	Disbursements	Profit/(Loss)	Organisation Expenses	Net Profit
1921	£692,897	£570,992	£121,905	£51,311	£70,594
1922	£862,401	£918,599	(£56,198)	£70,125	(£126,323)
1923	£1,323,726	£1,081,638	£242,088	£110,578	£131,510
1924	£1,567,922	£983,899	£584,023	£245,224	£338,779
1925	£1,641,024	£997,595	£643,429	£227,966	£415,463
1926	£1,588,480	£960,692	£627,788	£228,147	£399,641
1927	£1,593,245	£1,034,746	£558,499	£249,059	£309,440
1928	£1,616,780	£827,742	£789,038	£277,094	£511,944

1929	£1,629,377	£822,652	£806,725	£279,272	£527,453
1930	£1,029,605	£715,933	£313,672	£219,126	£94,546
1931	£545,251	£433,257	£111,994	£142,563	(£30,569)
1932	£711,929	£535,257	£176,672	£221,508	(£44,836)
1933	£563,804	£561,404	£2,400	£190,134	(£187,734)
1934	£605,266	£605,870	(£604)	£175,988	(£176,592)
1935	£673,590	£529,808	£143,782	£144,522	(£740)
1936	£611,179	£547,248	£63,931	£116,262	(£52,331)
1937	£745,470	£586,509	£158,961	£122,934	£36,027
1938 (est.)	£142,587	£184,345	(£41,758)	£25,335	(£67,093)
Total	£18,144,533	£12,898,186	£5,246,347	£3,097,148	£2,149,199

MAJESTIC

Year	Receipts	Disbursements	Profit/(Loss)	Organisation Expenses	Net Profit
1922	£1,143,648	£718,147	£425,501	£92,979	£332,522
1923	£1,639,515	£1,093,927	£545,588	£136,900	£408,688
1924	£1,678,455	£1,007,805	£670,650	£262,510	£408,140
1925	£1,195,013	£797,877	£397,136	£165,987	£231,149
1926	£1,787,784	£1,085,704	£702,080	£256,726	£445,354
1927	£1,691,518	£1,020,423	£671,095	£264,384	£406,711
1928	£1,572,377	£885,218	£687,159	£269,505	£417,654
1929	£1,584,816	£903,684	£681,132	£271,637	£409,495
1930	£1,156,259	£836,813	£319,446	£246,052	£73,394
1931	£652,072	£604,811	£47,261	£170,517	(£123,256)
1932	£712,919	£675,358	£37,561	£221,789	(£184,228)
1933	£541,330	£639,261	(£97,931)	£182,536	(£280,467)

1934	£528,198	£611,375	(£83,177)	£117,988	(£201,165)
1935	£615,761	£538,900	£76,861	£131,405	(£54,544)
1936	£134,362	£134,495	(£135)	£26,361	(£26,494)
Total	£16,634,027	£11,553,798	£5,080,229	£2,817,276	£2,262,953

APPENDIX 5

MAJESTIC PASSENGER STATISTICS

As one of the most popular ships afloat in the 1920s and '30s – indeed *the* most popular ship afloat for several years – *Majestic*'s yearly passenger carryings were impressive, as recorded by the North Atlantic Passenger Conference's tables:[1]

Year	Round trips	Passengers carried	Average per crossing	Cumulative total of passengers	Cumulative average per crossing
1922	10	26,370	1,319	26,370	1,319
1923	14½	36,779	1,268	63,149	1,289
1924	14	34,270	1,224	97,419	1,265
1925	12	28,630	1,193	126,049	1,248
1926	15½	37,800	1,219	163,849	1,241
1927	14½	37,822	1,304	201,671	1,253
1928	16	37,949	1,186	239,620	1,242
1929	14	34,894	1,246	274,514	1,242
1930	15½	28,978	935	303,492	1,204
1931	13	16,345	629	319,837	1,150
1932	17	18,051	531	337,888	1,083
1933	16	13,573	424	351,461	1,022
1934	15½	15,465	499	366,926	978
1935	15½	19,586	632	386,512	952
1936	4	3,146	393	389,658	941

Overall, *Majestic*'s average of 941 passengers carried on each crossing throughout her career was impressive; *Berengaria*'s average was a shade lower at 911 passengers per crossing in the same period. *Berengaria* carried an average of 980 passengers from 1923 to 1932 (on 300 crossings); *Leviathan* carried an average of 1,035 passengers in the same period (on 264 crossings), whereas *Majestic* averaged 1,067 passengers per crossing in the same period (on 292 crossings). As Frank Braynard noted, all three won in their own way: *Berengaria* carried a total of 430,395 passengers from 1921 to 1938, more than either of her younger running mates and over a longer period; *Leviathan* carried 40,539 passengers in 1927, the best single yearly total; *Majestic* carried more passengers than her sisters in several years, as well as having a higher average number of passengers on each crossing, in general.

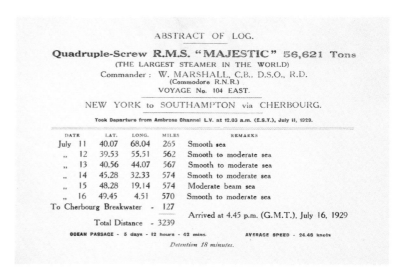

One example of hundreds of souvenir 'abstract of log' cards issued to passengers. This one recorded *Majestic*'s 104th eastbound crossing from New York to Southampton via Cherbourg. She encountered smooth or moderate seas and performed well, averaging about 24.5 knots with an obliging current. It tells us that she left New York and passed the Ambrose Channel Light Vessel just after midnight. She arrived at Cherbourg in the late afternoon of 16 July 1929. (Author's collection)

NOTES

Chapter 1

1 Braynard, Frank, *Classic Ocean Liners Volume 1: Berengaria, Leviathan & Majestic* (Patrick Stephens Ltd, 1990), p.7.
2 Broeze, F., 'Albert Ballin, The Hamburg-Bremen Rivalry and the Dynamics of the Conference System', *International Journal of Maritime History*, June 1991, vol. 3 no. 1, pp.19–20.
3 Warren, Mark D., *Shipbuilder Volume 2: 1907–14* (Blue Riband Publications, 1997), p.225, 262.
4 Broeze op. cit., p.25.
5 Broeze, op. cit., pp.24–5.
6 Broeze, op. cit., p.26.

Chapter 2

1 'The World's Largest Steamship', *Scientific American*, 23 May 1914; see also Isherwood, J.H., 'The *Vaterland* of 1914' (*Sea Breezes*, June 1964).
2 I am grateful to Michael Schneider for supplying information from Dr Foerster's own text, in: Dr-Ing. E. Foerster, G. Sütterlin: Der Vierschrauben-Turbinendampfer *Vaterland*, Verlag des VDI, 1918; and see '*Majestic* – The Latest and Largest of Ships', *Scientific American*, July 1922, p.10; also Braynard, vol. 1.
3 Braynard, vol. 1, pp.46–7.
4 Warren, p.221, p.304.

Chapter 3

1 Coleman, T., *The Liners* (Penguin Books, 1976), pp.105–106.
2 See Louden-Brown, P., *The White Star Line: An Illustrated History 1869–1934*, Titanic Historical Society, 2001, p.114.

Chapter 4

1 The title of 'commodore' was often used in an informal sense. For example, Captain Edward John ('E.J.') Smith (1850–1912) commanded a succession of White Star's largest ships before the war, from *Baltic* (1904) to *Adriatic* (1907) and *Olympic* (1911), before his final command *Titanic* (1912). He was sometimes referred to as commodore but the title was out of official use.
2 Hayes, B., *Hull Down* (Cassell & Co., 1925), pp.277–83.
3 Jordan, H., *Mauretania: Landfalls and Departures of Twenty-Five Years* (Patrick Stephens Limited, 1988), p.251.
4 Jordan, p.253.
5 *Berengaria* carried 29,907 passengers in 1923, while *Leviathan* carried 23,904 in 1924 and *Olympic* carried 24,991 passengers in 1924. (*Classic Ocean Liners*, p.47; Braynard, vol. 3, p.261.)
6 'Strakes' were essentially longitudinal (fore and aft) hull plating, the 'sheer strake' being the top strake of the side of the structural hull, while the 'stringer plates' were the outer strake of deck plating. See: Elijah Baker, *Introduction to Steel Shipbuilding*, 2nd edn (McGraw-Hill Book Company, 1943), pp.122–125. Braynard, vol.3, pp.182–3 offers a detailed analysis.

Chapter 5

1 Braynard, vol. 3, p.205.
2 Braynard, vol. 3, p. 261.
3 Braynard, vol. 3, p.244.
4 Altogether the three ships carried over 76,000 passengers in 1927; *Majestic* led with 37,822, while *Olympic* carried an impressive 24,405 passengers and *Homeric* over 14,000 passengers.
5 *Majestic*'s log recorded:
    3.12 p.m.: Speed 75 revs.
    3.20 p.m.: Heavy sea broke on board, No.1 hatches D and E decks stove in, forward third class passenger accommodation flooded (passengers moved to Tourist class aft) and various extensive damage done on forward decks. Engines dead slow. Wind: WNW, force 9.

Chapter 6

1 Quoted with permission from Halifax Herald Ltd.
2 Haws, D., *Merchant Fleets Volume 19: White Star Line (Oceanic Steam Navigation Company)* (TCL Publications, 1990), pp.22–3.
3 Ibid., p.23.
4 John Havers, 'White Star and Me', *Black Jack*, winter 1980–81, pp.5–6.

Chapter 7

1 Havers, pp.5–6.
2 *Berengaria* was withdrawn from service in spring 1938 due to the deteriorating condition of her wiring, while *Leviathan* went to the scrappers the same year – having made her last Atlantic voyage in 1934. By 1939, only *Majestic* was still in service – albeit as a training ship rather than a passenger liner.
3 Louden-Brown, p.114.

Appendix 4

1 The memo for each ship was entitled 'Financial Results of Operating'. The *Berengaria* figures were dated 8 December 1938 and the *Majestic* figures 19 December 1938. The figures were produced in order to compare the two ships' financial performance and were intended to be directly comparable, although some expenses for *Berengaria* in 1938 were estimates.
    A summary derived from White Star records provided a breakdown for 1931 that showed *Majestic*'s total revenues of £620,182 and disbursements of £546,486 (a gross profit of £73,696), but there is a variation with other figures produced by Cunard. Dated 7 November 1932, a document entitled 'SS *Majestic*'s Voyage Results Under Partnership Agreement: Profit Or Losses Included In Cunard Company's Accounts' gave a detailed listing of *Majestic*'s gross financial results from 1922 to 1931, which showed *Majestic*'s earnings in 1931 as £665,671, but her disbursements at £682,577 – resulting in a gross loss of £16,906 rather than a gross profit of £73,696. That documentation, too, showed figures slightly different from the figures shown in the December 1938 analysis of *Berengaria* and *Majestic* (which puts the gross profit as £47,261 in 1931). Financial data often varied slightly by source or were perhaps subject to revision by the accountants, but the trends are consistent. (See also Chirnside, Mark, *RMS Olympic: Titanic's Sister* [History Press, 2015], p.332.)

Appendix 5

1 The 1936 figure is taken from Cunard White Star's own records, and not those of the conference. While the number of round trips is accurate according to the conference, there may always be a slight discrepancy between the conference records and other sources due to rounding in any given year. As can be seen, the number of round trips in the table above add up to the 207 round trips that *Majestic* completed between 1922 and 1936.

BIBLIOGRAPHY

PUBLISHED SOURCES

Beaumont, J.C.H., *Ships and People* (Geoffrey Bles, 1926).

Bowyer, George, 'Lively Ahoy: Reminiscences of 58 Years in the Trinity House Pilotage Service' (H.B. Broadbere, 1930).

Braynard, Frank, *Classic Ocean Liners Volume 1: Berengaria, Leviathan & Majestic* (Patrick Stephens Ltd, 1990).

Braynard, Frank, *Leviathan: The World's Greatest Ship* (South Street Seaport Museum, 1974–83).

Chirnside, Mark, *RMS Aquitania: The 'Ship Beautiful'* (The History Press, 2008).

Chirnside, Mark, 'RMS *Majestic* to HMS *Caledonia*: The "Magic Stick's" Third Life' (*Voyage*, 2008).

Chirnside, Mark, *RMS Olympic: Titanic's Sister* (The History Press, 2015).

Coleman, Terry, *The Liners* (Penguin Books, 1976).

Foerster, Dr Ernst, 'Big and Fast Liners of the Future' (*Scientific American*, April 1923).

Foerster, Dr E., *Der Vierschrauben-Turbinendampfer Vaterland* (Verlag des VDI, 1918).

Haas, Charles A., '"Queen of the Western Ocean": White Star's Marvellous *Majestic*' (*Titanic Commutator*, summer 1978).

Havers, John, 'White Star and Me' (*Black Jack*, winter 1980–81).

Haws, Duncan, *Merchant Fleets Volume 19: White Star Line (Oceanic Steam Navigation Company)* (TCL Publications, 1990).

Hayes, Bertram, *Hull Down* (Cassell & Co., 1925).

Hoffman, Ross J.S., *Great Britain and the German Trade Rivalry 1875–1900* (Oxford University Press, 1933).

Isherwood, J. H., 'The *Vaterland* of 1914' (*Sea Breezes*, June 1964).

Isherwood, J. H., 'White Star Liner *Majestic* of 1922' (*Sea Breezes*, July 1968).

Jordan, Humfrey, *Mauretania: Landfalls and Departures of Twenty-Five Years* (Patrick Stephens Limited, 1988).

Louden-Brown, Paul, *The White Star Line: An Illustrated History 1869–1934* (Titanic Historical Society, 2001).

'*Majestic* – The Latest and Largest of Ships' (*Scientific American*, July 1922).

McAuley, Rob, *The Liners: A Voyage of Discovery* (Boxtree, 1997).

Robson, Tom, *Boy Seaman RN: The True Story* (Newton Press, 1996).

Streater, Les, *Berengaria: Cunard's 'Happy Ship'* (Tempus Publishing, 2001).

Warren, Mark D., *Shipbuilder Volume 2: 1907–14* (Blue Riband Publications, 1997).

Wilson, J. Lyell, 'The SS *Leviathan*, Damage, Repairs and Strength Analysis' (Transactions, SNAME 1930).

ARCHIVAL SOURCES

Archiv Internationales Maritimes Museum Hamburg

Ballin, Albert, to von Karpff, Herrn Kapitan, 12 October 1915. D26_163.

Cunard Archive, Sydney Jones Library, Liverpool University

D42/AC14/79/7; D42/ASC/12/3; D42/ASC/12/4a & b, ASC 14/82/2, D42/C1/296, C3/15, D42/GM8/1/27,30 & 32, GM 12/14, D302/1/9.

Merseyside Maritime Museum

B/CUN/8/1922.9/1/1; Information File, Steamships: K-W Vol. 2.

National Museums Scotland (National War Museum, Edinburgh Castle)

Braddock, Commander Walter, (Royal Navy Retired), 'The Final Days and Evacuation of HMS *Caledonia*.' (M2003.92.8).

Hazell, W. Douglas, 'The *Majestic Caledonia* Years (1937 to 1939).'

United Kingdom National Archives (formerly the Public Record Office)

ADM 1/9562; ADM 220/1426; CUST 130/116; MT 15/441; MT15/573; T161/1113.